THE TENT GENERATIONS

PALESTINIAN POEMS

T0383033

THE TENT GENERATIONS

PALESTINIAN POEMS

Selected, introduced
and translated from the Arabic by

Mohammed Sawaie

Banipal Books

The Tent Generations, Palestinian Poems
First published in English translation
by Banipal Books, London, 2022

Arabic copyright © the poets & their estates, 2022
English translation copyright © Mohammed Sawaie, 2022
Introduction Copyright © Mohammed Sawaie, 2022

A CIP record for this book is available in the British Library
ISBN 978-1-913043-18-6
E-book: ISBN: 978-1-913043-19-3

Front cover painting "Melancholic Homeland"
by Toufic Abdul-Al (1938–2002)

Banipal Books
1 Gough Square, LONDON EC4A 3DE, UK
www.banipal.co.uk/banipalbooks/

Banipal Books is an imprint of Banipal Publishing
Typeset in Cardo

Printed and bound in Great Britain by Clays Ltd, Elcograf S.p.A.

For all those who fight for justice and equality

CONTENTS

INTRODUCTION

This collection gathers a select number of twentieth-century Palestinian poets who give expression to the Palestinian experience under Israeli rule as well as the experience of dispersion of the Palestinian population from their homeland ensuing from the 1948 Arab-Israeli War and the subsequent wars of 1967 and 1973. All these tragic conflicts contributed to the loss of homeland, life under occupation, and the fragmentation of society and community. Through the work of the poets translated in this anthology, my goal is to illuminate Palestinian responses to the Israeli-Palestinian conflict, which has spawned competing narratives of belonging and blame in both Palestinian and Israeli cultures.

It should be noted that poetry has had an extremely high status among other cultural productions in Arab culture. Poetry arises for a variety of occasions; it is not some rarified genre of literature, but one with some mass appeal to a variety of audiences and readerships. More than other literary genres, poetry has played a similar role among Palestinians in Israel, and it is characterized as a product created spontaneously in reaction to events. Poetic themes, as evidenced by this anthology, are very much linked to historical, political and cultural changes before and after 1948.

The poetry belongs to a larger body of literature encompassing a variety of genres that deal with experiences suffered by

Palestinians. While these poems cannot hope to resolve the deep contradictions and disagreements that divide Palestinians and Israelis today, it is my hope to show how Palestinian poets in this collection have used poetry to describe their relationship to the Palestinian people, their homeland, and the presence of an Israeli adversary in their midst. The following overview briefly reflects on the social and cultural life of those Palestinians who remained in Israel in 1948, numbering about 160,000, and provides the context for the collection.[1] It is beyond the scope of this work to provide a detailed social, cultural, and political life of Palestinians in the diaspora.

As a consequence of the 1948 Arab-Israeli War and the establishment of the state of Israel, the majority of Palestinians, whether villagers or city dwellers, men and women of letters, and those with education and other professional skills fled, or were forced to leave their places of residence. Cities such as Jaffa, Haifa, Akka (Acre), among others, were the centers of political leadership, journalism, educational institutions, and culture. Poets and intellectuals like Abd al-Karim al-Karmi, popularly known by the agnomen Abu Salma, Muhammad al-Adnani, Hasan al-Buhayri, Mahmoud al-Afghani, Harun Hashim Rasheed, Burhan al-Din al-Abushi, and many others became refugees in neighboring Arab countries. Cities such as Jaffa, a metropolis of approximately 100,000 Palestinian inhabitants before 1948, were flourishing centers of culture, commerce, education, journalism, printing presses, social and sports clubs, health institutions, women's organizations, and political activities. Once a prospering city, Jaffa suddenly became a place where only several thousand impoverished Palestinians assembled to live in a ghetto after 1948. Many of those new

2

inhabitants were destitute internal refugees who converged in the city from neighboring villages and rural communities that were destroyed by Israeli forces. Arab Palestinians in Israel became isolated under Israeli rule, cut off politically, culturally, and educationally from other Palestinians outside the Israeli borders at that time, as well as from other Arabs generally.

The state of war that endured between Israel and the Arab countries compounded the cultural and geographical isolation of the Arab Palestinians, adding to their misery. Moreover, the suffering of this Palestinian minority in Israel deteriorated under the imposition of military rule from 1948 until 1966. This harsh regime gave state, regional, and local military governors authority to confiscate more Arab land, to suppress fundamental human rights such as freedom of expression and political association, to restrict freedom of movement, to deny employment, to impose house arrest, as well as to banish Palestinian citizens to other localities at will for any perceived infringement of military rule.[2] At times, the extent of this iron-fisted military administration reached the absurd, Kafkaesque level of even criminalizing individuals for purchasing the newspaper *al-Ittihad*, whose publishing was sanctioned by the state.[3]

Few of those Palestinians who remained in Israel in 1948 were teachers, writers, or journalists.[4] For example, in 1949 only fifty Palestinian Arabs with a university education remained in Israel. (Their academic degrees had presumably been obtained at universities outside Palestine before 1948.)[5] Despite the economic hardships, the military restrictions, and the forced separation from their compatriots and other Arabs, those few teachers, journalists, and writers suddenly found themselves burdened with immense responsibilities. They were compelled to assume the role of defenders of and spokespersons for the rights of this small Arab minority. Few poets and writers emerged from among this Palestinian minority, yet in the midst of this dark cultural and political situation, a new light came forth.

Although Palestinian poets in Israel had limited venues to disseminate their creations and faced hardships and limited access to printing facilities, a few anthologies were published, albeit in crude editions paid for by the poets themselves. Poet and author Fahd Abu Khadra presents a partial study of the first stage of Palestinian poetry in Israel, extending from 1948 to 1958, which is characterized by the creation of anthologies.[6] He claims that there was an abundance of Palestinian poetry. The published anthologies, he asserts, represent only a small portion of the poems that appeared in newspapers and journals. In his view, poems by Palestinians that appeared in the press number in the thousands. They could amount to volumes, provided they were easily accessible. During the period of his study, Abu Khadra counted eight collections, diwans as they are referred to in Arabic. The first was by George Najib Khalil (1932–2001), titled *Ward wa Qatad* [Roses and Thorns] published in 1953, five years after the establishment of the state of Israel.[7] This anthology was followed a year later by another titled *'Ahlam Ha'ir* [Dreams of a Perplexed Man] by Isa Lubani. Michel Iskandar Haddad, editor of a journal by the title of *al-Mujtama'*, published *'Alwan min al-Shi'r al-'Arabi fi Israel* in 1955, an anthology comprising poems by seventeen contributors, four of whom were recent Arabic-speaking Jewish immigrants from Iraq.[8] Haddad's collection contains both experienced authors and novices just starting out

4

as writers and poets; some of the names of the contributors did not resurface beyond his anthology. The poems follow, with few exceptions, the traditional, classical format of the poem in Arabic, and adhere to one meter throughout the poem. Two hemistichs comprise each line, and the second half ends with the same rhyme. The poems are mostly lyrics dealing with personal themes, with titles such as "First Love", "Hope", "Regret", "To the Dark Lady", "Kiss Me", "Come Back to Me", and so on. Political issues facing Palestinians there at the time, or those outside Israel, were avoided generally, either because of the interference of the heavy-handed Israeli censor, or out of fear of punishment by the harsh military rule at the time.

Besides publishing anthologies at their own expense, Palestinian poets and other writers had alternative venues for disseminating their writings. These included publication by cooperating with Israeli governmental agencies or publishing through political parties that enjoyed state financial support. The support provided by government agencies and political parties, for example, was motivated by a desire to reach a wide swath of speakers of Arabic, Palestinians as well as Arabic-speaking Jews who had migrated from Arab countries. For example, the newspaper *al-Yawm* [Today] was established as a daily in Jaffa in October 1948 as the organ for the views of the influential Zionist Labor Mapai, the leading force in the 1948 War, which was in charge of the state for many years after its foundation.[9] The United Workers Party, Mapam, supported other Arabic publications, an example being the literary monthly *al-Fajr* [Dawn] established in Fall 1958. The Palestinian poets Rashid Hussein and George Najib Khalil were the editors of the literary section and the editorial secretary of this paper, respectively. *Al-*

Fajr came under attack in some Jewish circles; however, its Arab editors were accused of publishing articles and poems in praise of Arab national themes. The charges of chauvinistic Arab nationalism directed against the editors eventually resulted in the closure of the paper in Fall 1962.[10]

Affiliation with the Israeli Communist Party enabled its Arab members to initiate talks with Israeli communists aimed at giving Palestinians a degree of voice, and some publications arose as a result of this affiliation.[11] Thus, the Palestinian members of the Communist Party were able to re-establish in October 1948 the newspaper *al-Ittihad*, which was first published in the city of Haifa in May 1944 as the mouthpiece of the Palestinian 'Usbat al-Taharrur al-Watani, League of National Emancipation, (a branch of the Arab Communist Party), and had been closed by the British Mandate authorities in January 1948. *Al-Ittihad* resumed publishing on October 18, 1948 as the weekly Arabic supplement to the Hebrew newspaper 'al Hamishmar. *Al-Jadid*, first issued in 1951 as a monthly literary and cultural supplement to *al-Ittihad*, was published as an independent literary and cultural journal in 1953. This publication opened its pages to the leading Palestinian poets and writers, regardless of their party affiliation. Among its contributors were the poets and writers Rashid Hussein, George Najib Khalil, Emil Habibi, Isam Abbasi, Hanna Abu Hanna, among many others. Contributors to *al-Jadid* also included several Arabic-speaking Jewish immigrants from Iraq such as Shimon Ballas, David Semah, Sasson Somekh, to name only a few.[12] Both publications served as major forums for Palestinian literary and cultural production. Furthermore, they were instrumental in raising issues of national identity among Palestinians in Israel.

Other venues available to Palestinian poets and writers were organizations that promoted poetry and Palestinian culture as well as Arab identity, such as Rabitat Shu'ara' al-'Arabiyya, The League of Arabic Poets, formed in March 1954. This was followed in March 1955 by Rabitat al-Qalam al-Arabi, The League of the Arab Pen, and, finally, Rabitat al-'udaba' wa al-Muthaqqafin al-Arab, The League of Arab Intellectuals, formed in September 1957. None of these organizations lasted long, however, because of political and ideological differences between their members, which translated into different goals and strategies. At the same time, they were under pressure from an ever-present sword of Damocles, the Israeli military rule.[13]

Access to print materials such as newspapers decreased with growing poverty and structural challenges to literacy among Palestinians who remained in Israel at the time of the establishment of the state in 1948. Books were scarce and hard to find due to the closure of borders. Consequently, poets resorted to another strategy to disseminate their poetry. Arab culture has traditionally placed emphasis on reciting poetry, on listening to it in a communal setting. Poems were customarily memorized, passed on from one individual to another and from one generation to the next. Among Palestinians in Israel, poetic festivals or *mahrajans*, were a means to connect poetry with the wider public, whose access to print was limited.[14] At those festivals, held in cities such as Haifa, Nazareth, Akka (Acre), as well as in small and remote villages, poets often appealed to the emotions of the crowds, to their hopes for freedom, to their struggle for rights, while affirming their Palestinian identity. These poetry mahrajans eventually morphed into literary and political demonstrations. Beyond this, *mahrajans* formed an important political and social factor by boosting the morale of Palestinians in Israel, raising their confidence, and extending support to national and political issues.

These festivals provided poets with opportunities to be close to people, to influence them politically through their poems, and to be influenced by them. Poems delivered in those festivals were generally in the traditional format of Arabic poetry, suitable for oration, easy to recite and to remember. Poets derived some of their diction from the everyday language of the people and often referred to current events. This poetry manifested hope, optimism, and the will to continue the struggle for rights and freedom. Yet poems recited in those *mahrajans* also dealt with issues that generate sadness, pain, and exposed issues of discrimination and confinement. They also decried the misery of the lives of other Palestinian compatriots separated from them, living in abjection and forcibly in refugee camps outside their native homeland. Israeli newspapers criticized the holding of those festivals. The Israeli police and other intelligence-gathering agencies tried to stop them, and also to stop poets from reaching the appointed festival sites.[15] These efforts were not successful, however: group poetry recitation continues to this day, whether at cultural functions in annual book fairs in Arab cities, summer festivals, or in political gatherings, large or small.

Palestinian poets belong to two groups, based on the themes and formal features of their poetry. George Najib Khalil, Isa Lubani, Jamal Qa'war, Mahmoud Mustafa Dessouki, and a few others belong to the first generation of Palestinian poets inside Israel, writing lyrics on subjective themes, and adhering to meters and rhymes as espoused by the classical, traditional poem structure. In the early 1960s, a second generation of Palestinian poets, some of whom were contemporary with poets in this first generation, pioneered writing, mostly in the new format of *shi'r al-taf'ila*, often referred to as *al-shi'r al-hurr*, "free verse", introduced into modern Arabic poetry-writing around the mid 1940s by poets from Iraq. Poems written in free verse are characterized by an agility of expression and freedom from classical poetry's rigid structure that requires adherence to one meter and rhyme.

Despite various claims over who pioneered the free-verse movement in modern Arabic poetry, there is consensus, however, that the Iraqi poets Badr Shakir al-Sayyab, Nazik al-Mala'ika and Abdel Wahab al-Bayati spearheaded the movement. Claims are also made to the effect that Ali Ahmad Bakathir, originally from South Yemen, preceded these Iraqi poets in writing plays using free verse. Still other critics argue that Arabic poetry had diverged much earlier from al-Khalil ibn Ahmed al-Farahidi's guidelines for classical poems, as evidenced by poetry by Abu Nuwas and others during the Abbasid era, and also by the Andalusian *muwashshahs* that introduced varying patterns of rhyme in poems and structures. Once free verse gained respectability in literary circles, however, it won the day despite opposition by voices that judged it to be illegitimate. It should be noted that poets such as Tawfiq Zayyad (1929-1994), Samih al-Qasim (1939-2014), and Salem Jubran (1941-2012) wrote in traditional forms, yet the bulk of their poetry is in free verse.[16]

This second generation not only transformed the structure of verse, but also shifted the focus of poetry from subjective lyrics to topics of concern to Palestinian Arabs as a national minority in Israel. Expressions of defiance and the assertion of national identity became the emphasis of this poetry. Poets engaged in writing nationalistic poetry were following in the footsteps of earlier Palestinian poets in the 1930s and 1940s as represented by Abd al-Rahim Mahmoud (1913-1948), Ibrahim Tuqan (1905-1941), Abu Salma (1906-1980), and others who wrote poetry in opposition to British rule over Palestine in the period from 1917 until 1948, as well as against perceived Zionist plans for establishing a Jewish national homeland in Palestine.

This second generation of Palestinian poets, who came of age under Israeli rule, rose to defend their rights as citizens of the state, to oppose harsh military rule and rulers, to protest the detention of citizens, restrictions on their movement, arbitrary imprisonment, and to defend freedom of speech. The themes that characterize their poetry include a yearning for freedom, for equality with other citizens of the state, and solidarity for the rights of their own people outside the borders of the state, with whom they lost contact in 1948. Furthermore, they wrote in support of other nations, for example, Cuba, Vietnam, Algeria, and other African colonies. Among the representatives of this second group of poets, the following deserve special mention: Samih al-Qasim (1939-2014), Mahmoud Darwish (1941-2008), Rashid Hussein (1936-1977), Salem Jubran (1941-2011), Hanna Abu Hanna (1928-2022), and Tawfiq Zayyad (1929-1994), to name only a few. Their voices address people in the collective, speaking of the pain of victimization, expressing their desire for love of humanity and opposition to the prevalence of injustice, and a longing for the restoration of rights and desire for peace. They were guided by hope, despite all the hardships meted out to them and their fellow citizens: the confiscation of their writings, censorship, house arrests, imprisonments, and expulsion from employment.

These poets believed struggle would initiate an end to their misery; "the sun will rise again," as one of them expressed. Rashid Hussein, for instance, introducing his anthology *Ma' al-Fajr* [At Dawn], published in 1957, wrote the following while addressing his Palestinian compatriots: "Brethren: I gathered my pains and yours, invited my joys and yours, dissolved my love and yours and then I gathered all of this in the cauldron of my soul." Samih al-Qasim introduced his first anthology, *Mawakib al-Shams* [Procession of the Sun], published in 1958, as follows: "The sun has risen from behind the dreadful, dark mountains weighing heavily on the bosom of our east. Our mighty sun has started rolling in the sky of our land, shattering those mountains." Mahmoud Darwish introduced his first anthology, *'Asafir bila 'Ajniha* [Birds Without Wings], which he completed while in prison and published in 1960, by writing the following: "In August and September the world has crowded my life . . . love . . . suffering . . . struggle and revolution, pain and the harsh call approaching from afar." Finally, Mahmoud Mustafa Dessouki (1934-2015) introduced his anthology, *Mawakib al-Ahrar* [Procession of the Free], published in 1963, with the following words: "to march forward on the road of struggle to remove the yoke of oppression from our necks and to realize our full rights in order to live free, liberated, with full dignity in the land of our fathers and forefathers."[17]

Several events in neighboring Arab countries in the mid to late 1950s impacted Arab Palestinians in Israel, especially poets. These events raised awareness of their connectedness to, and solidarity with other Arabs outside the confines of the borders of the state of Israel. For example, the invasion of Egypt by

Britain, France, and Israel in October-November 1956, generally referred to as the Suez War, ignited solidarity with Egypt. Many poems were written against the aggressors and destruction caused by this conflict, especially about the Egyptian city of Port Said that bore the brunt of that invasion. On the eve of this war, a horrendous event touched the lives of Palestinians in Israel in particular, and other Arabs in general—a catastrophe that had an immense impact on poetry production.

On October 29, 1956, forty-nine Palestinians, including women and children of all ages, were massacred in the village of Kufr Qasim by Israeli border police. These villagers were returning to their village from working in fields and other places, unaware of a curfew that Israel had imposed at 4:30 to be effective at 5:00 on that same day. Many Palestinian and other Arab poets, outraged by this massacre, commemorated this occasion by penning soul-searching poems, including the one in this volume. Countering those gloomy events were two that boosted national feelings among Palestinians in Israel, and generated poems expressing hope for freedom and deliverance from the Israeli yoke. The first was the declaration of the union between Egypt and Syria in February 1958; the second was the revolution in Iraq and the ouster of the pro-West royal family in July 1958.[18]

These epochal events inspired the production of various literary genres, most noticeably poetry. Almost a decade later, the 1967 Arab-Israeli June War resulted in Arab defeat. This defeat, referred to as *naksa*, "set back", had many grave consequences: more Arab lands came under occupation by Israel, thus resulting in more refugees, especially Palestinians who took refuge in neighboring countries. The significant result was more human misery—and suffering that found expression in poetry. The seizure of the Palestinian West Bank by the Israeli army in 1967 broke down the sealed barriers that had been established in 1948. This new situation enabled the Palestinian communities in Israel to renew contact with their brethren and members of families residing in the West Bank. The themes of war, suffering and reacquaintance stirred latent poetic expression, inspiring numerous volumes of poetry by Palestinian poets in Israel, as represented by Mahmoud Darwish, Samih al-Qasim, Tawfiq Zayyad, Salem Jubran, Rashid Hussein, among many others, as well as by Palestinian poets living in the West Bank and the diaspora.

The Palestinian poets included in *The Tent Generations* represent different age groups and backgrounds, yet they all express a strong sense of "Palestinian-ness". They include Israeli citizens, the offspring of those who remained in Palestine after 1948. They also include poets who lived or continue to live in the West Bank and Gaza, areas that are still occupied, or controlled by Israelis as of this writing. Finally, they include poets born in Palestine, but whose families were expelled, or migrated to neighboring Arab countries as a result of the Arab-Israeli wars of 1948, 1967, and 1973.

The educational backgrounds of the poets represented here also vary. Salem Jubran, Samih al-Qasim, Tawfiq Zayyad, and Marwan Makhoul, for example, were products of the Israeli educational system. Others attended institutions of learning in various Arab countries. Fadwa Tuqan received little formal education in her city of Nablus; she, however, acquired instruction in language, support in writing poetry, and encouragement to publish her poems from her brother, the well-known poet Ibrahim Tuqan, mentioned previously.

All these poems are written in *fusha* Arabic, Modern Standard Arabic, the codified literary, written language shared by educated speakers of Arabic in their various respective regions. Palestinian folkloric poetry, referred to as *al-Shi'r al-Sha'bi* or *Shi'r al-'Ammiyya*, is not included in this work. Folk poetry, richly expressed orally in the Palestinian dialect, *'ammiyya*, embraces a variety of themes (national pride, panegyric, love, generosity toward guests/strangers, and so on), including the political themes expressed in the poems in this work. There is a rising interest in collecting and preserving this folkloric poetry, and several anthologies of oral poetry as well as studies have recently appeared.[19]

The uprooting of Palestinians from their ancestral homeland and their dispersal world-wide by the Israelis did not happen without resistance expressed in different forms, ranging from military to political activities to literary expressions in various genres, chief amongst them poetry. The works gathered in *The Tent Generations* also form part of a robust critical debate that began with Palestinian novelist and writer Ghassan Kanafani, who published a monograph in 1966 titled *'Adab al-Muqawama fi Filastin al-Muhtalla* [Resistance Literature in Occupied Palestine]. He also wrote *al-'Adab al-Filastini al-Muqawim taht al-Ihtilal 1948-1968* [Palestinian Literature of Resistance under Occupation 1948-1968]. In both works, Kanafani argues that Palestinian literary production, represented in poems, short stories, plays and other genres, is an expression of "resistance" to occupiers by people under occupation. This cultural production, according to Kanafani, connects social and political issues in intimate ways in order to effect change. Most importantly, poems express resistance to the Israeli occupation by demonstrating the poets and other creative writers' deep commitment to their homeland and to freedom. These works, according to Kanafani, expose the daily suffering of their compatriots who face imprisonment, the routine confiscation of their land, and who lack freedom.

The term *'Adab al-Muqawama*, "Resistance Literature", attributed to Kanafani and later adopted by others, acquired a significant presence in literary circles, especially in reference to literary production by Palestinian writers in Israel. In any case, we observe that the term is derived from the verb *qawama*, "to resist", especially in two earlier poems by Samih al-Qasim, and Mahmoud Darwish. *'Adab al-Muqawama* has established a trend; it has gained popularity, especially among Palestinian critics and writers, as well as among other Arab writers with deep sympathy and support for the Palestinian cause.[20] The periods of 1950s and 1960s, when Kanafani's works were published, were characterized by the ideology of commitment in the literary circles in the Arab world, a rally to commit to the cause of the people through the production of literature and other cultural genres. This support of all literary forms is referred to as *al-'iltizam*, a commitment to express and devote literary and cultural production to the issues facing the nation; to expose oppression; to get rid of the oppressor (be they colonial or local dictatorial rulers); to support the *fellahin*, "land tillers", against the feudal class, large-tract landowners; to extend a hand to the poor in their struggle to improve their circumstances; to support Palestinians against the Israeli denial of rights; and to support the oppressed in the world against the oppressor. This school of thought pointedly problematizes the idea of "art for art's sake".

The notion of *'Adab al-Muqawama* met with opposition in some quarters of Arab literary circles, as well as in others. The Egyptian critic Ghali Shukri, for example, argued in his book *'Adab al-Muqawama* [The Literature of Resistance] that the poetry written by Palestinian poets in Israel does not qualify as true poetry of resistance. In world literature, Shukri argued, resistance literature was associated, and equated with, the act of carrying arms against the occupier, as was the case in France during the Nazi occupation of the country in World War II, for example. Inasmuch as Palestinian poets in Israel did not engage in carrying arms, Shukri insisted, the term therefore could not aptly apply to their poetry. While Shukri's intention was not to belittle the importance of this literary production by these poets, he argued that poetry by Palestinian poets is more a poetry of *mu'arada*, of objection and opposition to those who rule over the Palestinians. These views are echoed by the poet and critic Ali Ahmad Said, popularly known as Adonis, who writes that what is referred to as resistance poetry is still, in his assessment, "missionary", appealing to the masses in the prevalent poetic language with its emotional and intellectual charge, using ordinary and traditional styles and methods. In Adonis's view, this is consumerist poetry that only offers delusion to its readers.[21] With regard to its development, Adonis states that resistance poetry is only an extension of Arabic poetry dealing with themes of nationalism and independence that appeared after World War I and continues to this day. Its distinctive feature is a Palestinian thematics. This "resistance poetry", according to Adonis, laments, sermonizes, expresses nostalgia, remembers places, describes, narrates—exactly like national Arabic poetry of the independence era or the earlier twentieth century.[22]

Such conflicting views have raised heated discussions in many quarters. The Israeli academic Shmuel Moreh, who migrated to Israel from Iraq in 1951, suggests that most critics of Arabic literature in Israel in general, and poetry in particular, were not objective in their treatment of this literature. They understood it as a means of propaganda in support of, or in opposition to political constellations. Palestinian poets and writers, Moreh maintains, expressed themselves and their problems in their own style, originating from their experiences, language, and real-life situations—warmly, honestly, forcefully, and freely. Yet, Moreh states, other Arab writers and critics erroneously called this literature "resistance literature", due to the fact that most of this literature is political, dealing with circumstances and events that would otherwise be forgotten with the passing of time. He maintains that the importance of poems and stories that deal with the sufferings resulting from Israeli military rule (1948-1966), for example, lost their significance once military rule was abolished.[23]

The Palestinian poet Mahmoud Darwish, himself once an Israeli citizen until his decamping in 1970 when he joined the ranks of the Palestine Liberation Organization, stated when asked about '*Adab al-Muqawama* that he did not care about the terminology nor the question. Through his poetry, Darwish views himself as a defender of his homeland against the occupier and denier of rights for his people, a literary defense against powers that oppress or seek to vanquish them. His writing reflects, in his view, the psychology of the person who rises to defend his homeland against strangers who seize the country by force and subjugate its indigenous population to dispersion and oppression. According to Darwish, his writing of poetry is a form of resistance to those who usurp his rights, his land, and his freedom. There is a need, he maintains, to redefine the meaning of resistance to include aspects deeper than instantaneous rejection and predictable reactions to oppression. "Is Palestinian poetry merely a reflection of such naïve reactions?" Darwish asks assertively. To him, the poetry of resistance includes *sumud*, steadfastness, rejection, real revolution, by equipping 'the writer' with knowledge and practice to change the status quo radically— even through revolution.[24] As Adonis observed about Palestinian poetry in 1969 in an article titled "Hawla al-shi'r wa al-thawra" [On Poetry and Revolution]:

> It is poetry of protest and of defense of usurped or oppressed freedom; a kind of counter cultural attack to the culture of occupation. This is why our poets in the occupied land acquire special significance . . . Palestinian poetry does not exhibit any racist attitudes . . . it does not exhibit a sense of superiority; it expresses human's deep connection to his [the poet's] land not apparent in all Arabic poetry . . . Land in this poetry is the alter ego of the person; it is his existential extension, the part the completes the whole.[25]

Notwithstanding the critical debate, poets still face repercussions for their work, as shown by the relatively recent case of Dareen Tatour, a Palestinian citizen of Israel, who posted a poem on YouTube whose title roughly translates as "Resist, my people, resist". The video resulted in her arrest and imprisonment in November 2015 for a three-month term; she was put under house arrest in 2016 in the Israeli city of Kiryat Ono, without access to the internet. The accusation of incitement to violence and supporting a "terrorist" organization was made against Tatour. On 31 July 2018, the poet was sentenced to five months in prison by the Israeli court in Nazareth. She was released on 20 September 2018 after completing the prison term.

The 1948 *Nakba*, the wars of 1967 and 1973, and their subsequent tragic impact find expression in the work of Palestinian poets. Some of the authors in this anthology had firsthand experience of the loss of home, and the uprootedness from and destruction of their villages and cities. Others acquired knowledge of such experiences, the tragedy that befell Palestinians, through stories told by grandparents or parents, stories of hardship and deprivation transmitted from one generation to another. Thus, poets express in vocabulary specific to the Palestinian experience of the dispossession of homeland, the forced expulsion, the pain of living in the miserable conditions of refugee camps in the diaspora. Not surprisingly, frequently occurring terms in this poetry are: "[refugee] camp", "misery and bitterness of life [in these camps]", "hunger", "exile", "homeland", "death", "sadness", and related terms. Words expressing "memory" and "remembrance", especially of the names of the poets' Palestinian cities and villages, and the yearning for those places or the homeland generally with all the topographical components as a marker of identity, reveal a deep commitment and adherence to the land and the struggle for it in the hopes of return, and to end to the dispersion of the uprooted, indigenous population that began with the establishment of the state of Israel in 1948. These discourses and intellectual perspectives are frequently used and encountered in the writings of Palestinian poets.

One may well ask how the poets and poems in this anthology

were selected. My selection, while certainly subjective in some degree, was guided by several factors: the desire to include poets, men and women who have not been introduced previously to English-speaking audiences, especially poets born in Palestine before the *Nakba* who matured in Israel after the establishment of the state in 1948. The poets in this anthology therefore span and represent different generations and different backgrounds. Mahmoud Darwish, for example, a prolific poet, is widely known in Western literary circles; his poetry has been translated into English and other languages. This explains why he is not included in this anthology. Similarly, Samih al-Qasim, has had a following in Western circles; some of his poetry has been translated into English as well as into other languages. Despite this, I introduce in this collection two poems by this poet. These two poems are lyrical, humorous, yet they possess sad tones that touch the heart of any person experiencing separation from family through imprisonment, or exile from a lost homeland. A few contemporary poets born outside Israel after the 1948 *Nakba* are also included.

Another important factor in the choice of poems in this collection is their translatability. Translating poetry presents problems at many levels, perhaps chief among which is the difficulty of locating the appropriate diction in the target language that conveys the nuances of the source. Different languages possess their own repertoires of imagery, systems of prosody, culture-specific allusions, and intertextuality. These differences add to the labor of the translator. Regardless of these difficulties, it is important to note that the choice of the poems in this work was largely based on the extent to which they can be translated in a manner allowing the English speaker to share their message as a universal human experience. In addition, poems were selected with imagery, humor, and irony that can bridge cultures. A final factor in the selection process was the desire to include poems whose content can be appreciated without the need for extensive footnotes.

The arrangement of the poets included in this collection and their poems follows chronological order, determined by generational progression of these poets, with respect to their poetry production and engagement with the Palestinian question.

Many of the poems included are likely to have appeared in newspapers, journals, and other means of dissemination, such as being recited at poetry readings or poetry *mahrajans* and festivals before being included in book format and poetry collections. Whenever possible, the date of composition or publication has been provided. To provide information reflecting the actual year the poems were authored, we found some instances where the poet dated his or her poem. We also relied on the dates when "complete works", or single anthologies were published—which do not necessarily provide the accurate date when each poem was authored. In those instances, the nearest approximate date (circa, c.) has been given; if there is no available date, the poem is marked (n.d.). Poets often did not date their poems, and for commercial reasons, publishers oftentimes compiled their works in tomes labelled "Complete Works". However, it has been found time and again that such labels often fall short of representing the true whole, complete production of poets. After the death of a poet, researchers often find material that was not included in "complete works" due to several reasons, including the negligence of poets to keep a complete record of their production, or censorship, whether self-imposed or for political or social reasons.

Many of the poems in this work address political issues. This subject matter may account for the flights of oratory and rhetoric, forged in the face of an adversary whose perceived goal was and still is to "tame", to "contain" and to "obliterate" the rebellious Arab citizen. Political discussion of their painful and tragic fate is the central preoccupation of Palestinians, especially the denial of their rights, and their continued maltreatment by friend and foe. Besides political themes, Palestinian poets write about varied themes like poets worldwide: descriptive, panegyric and elegiac poetry, and lyrics dealing with love, the universal human experience. This explains the inclusion of three amatory poems "To Eve" and "To a Visitor" by Salem Jubran, and "Christmas Misgivings" by Rita Odeh.

Finally, it should be mentioned that this anthology joins a constellation of other translated Palestinian poetry. The selected poems in this collection, however, introduce a considerable number of poets whose voices have not been heard previously in English, and, by and large, those not contained in previous works. In the few cases where there is overlap, my translation has been guided by the openness of the translation process, which grants literary works a different life with each new translation across time. This current work, in addition, includes poets of younger generations who are still active and today give voice to the Palestinian tragedy.

Introduction

NOTES

1 The number of Palestinians in Israel at the time of the establishment of the state varies, depending on the adopted date of the count: May 14, 1948, or April 1949, when additional Arab population was added due the acquisition of the Triangle Villages and their inhabitants after the Rhodes agreement between Jordan and Israel. Sabri Jiryis mentions that the number in 1949 was 160,000. Adel Manna', on the other hand, asserts that this number is overblown. The correct number around January 1949 was approximately 125,000, according to Manna'. See Sabri Jiryis, *The Arabs in Israel* (New York: Monthly Review Press, 1976), 289, and Adel Manna', *Nakba wa Baqa'* (Beirut: Mu'assast al-Dirasat al-Filastiniyya, 2016) ,131- 132.

2 Regarding the excesses of Israel's military rule, an Israeli governor was quoted as summarizing the practices against Palestinian citizens during those years: "[The military government] interferes in the life of Arab citizen from the day of his birth to the day of his death. It has the final say in all matters concerning workers, peasants, professional men, merchants, and educated men, with schooling and social services. It interferes in the registration of births, deaths, and even marriage, in questions of land and in the appointment and dismissal of teachers and civil servants. Often, too, it arbitrarily interferes in in the affairs of political parties, in political and social activities, and in local and municipal councils." Jiryis, *The Arabs in Israel*, 40.

3 *Al-Ittihad* was first established in Haifa in 1944 by 'Usbat al-Taharrur al-Watani as an organ of the Communist Party, was suspended by the British Mandate authorities in January 1948. However, it was re-issued as a weekly on October 18, 1948. As of 1954 it appeared twice a week, Tuesday and Friday. It is currently published in Haifa by *al-Jabha al-Dimoqratiyya li-al-Salam wa al-Musawa* ("The Democratic Front for Peace and Equality"). The famous Palestinian novelist Emil Habibi (1921-1996), the historian Emil Touma (1919-1987), and a few others were among *al-Ittihad*'s leading editors and writers. As for the claim of criminalizing the purchase of al-Ittihad, see Jubran, Sleman *Madkhal li-Dirasat al-Shi'r al-Filastini fi Israel, 1948-1967* in al-Hiwar al-Mutamaddin, issues nos. 3834 and 3839. See also Habeeb

23

Qahwaji, *al-Sihafa wa al-Mujtam' al-Isra'ili* (Damascus: Mu'assast al-Ard li-al-Dirasat al-Filistiniyya, 1974), 238-239.

4 In this environment teachers shouldered the heaviest burden. They were constantly under scrutiny by the Israeli Ministry of Education. Expulsion was practiced against any teacher, or anyone who expressed signs of national Palestinian sentiments and who showed a sign of dissent with the ministry of education, or the superintendent, or the school principal. The best teachers were expelled in 1949 and in 1952 in punishment for demanding better salaries, better work conditions, and professional organization. To replace them, the Israeli Ministry of Education appointed teachers with minimal education, individuals who had not even completed secondary school studies. Those dark years, education in Palestine suffered at many levels: a lack of instructional books for Arabs, untrained teachers, and the inadequacy of buildings, services, and equipment. See Jubran, Sleman, *Madkhal li-Dirasat al-Shi'r al-Filastini fi Israel 1948-1967*, (Nazareth: *Kul al-Arab* newspaper & al-Hiwar al-Mutamaddin, 2012 issue no. 3834); Jiryis, *The Arabs in Israel*, 203-214.

Hanna Abu Hanna, the Palestinian poet, teacher, and writer, reports that he was about to be engaged to a fellow teacher in the school in Israel where they both taught, when an agent of the military ruler threatened him that he would lose his job if they proceeded with the marriage plans, presumably because of his political views and activities. See Dina Matar, *What It Means to Be Palestinian: Stories of Palestinian Peoplehood* (London & New York: I. B. Taurus, 2010), 76.

It should also be noted that the abolishment of the military rule in 1966 did not result in putting an end to the suffering of Palestinians in Israel: their land was still subject to confiscation; poets and writers were subject to censorship and imprisonment, and members of the Knesset to banishment from this parliamentarian institution for expressing views that are not in line with the ruling government.

5 Jiryis, *The Arabs in Israel*, 209. Hebrew University in Jerusalem, established in 1925, adopted Hebrew as the language of instruction. No Palestinian Arab at the time was sufficiently skilled in Hebrew to enroll at this university.

6 Fahd Abu Khadra, 'al-Bunya al-Shakliyya fi al-Shi'ir al-Mahalli, al-Marhala al-'Uula' in Mahmoud Ghanayim (ed.), *Maraya fi al-Naqd*, (Kafr Qar', Israel: Markaz Dirasat al-Adab al-Arabi & Dar al-Huda, 2000), 15-34.

7 George Najib Khalil's *Ward wa Qatad*, "Roses and Thorns", was the first published poetry collection in1953, five years after the establishment of Israel

in 1948. The lyrical poems of *Ward wa Qatad* avoid discussion of politics; however, a few poems touch lightly some social issues. The poems in *Ward wa Qatad* cover three areas, arranged in three *babs*, "chapters": love, description of places in [historical] Palestine; in addition, there is a third "section" that deals with miscellaneous topics: solidarity with the working class, an anthem to May 1st [International Labor Day], women's education, obituary, importance of education, importance of patience, and such topics. Khalil provides glosses for words he assumes his readers would not understand, which supports the claim that Palestinians who remained in Israel in 1948 did not have advanced educations.

8 Michel Iskandar Haddad, *'Alwan min al-Shi'r al-Arabi fi Israel*, (Nazareth: Matba'at al-Hakim, 1955). Four of the seventeen poets in this collection are Iraqi Jews who were recent immigrants from Iraq.

9 *al-Yawm*, established in October 1948, expropriated the offices, the printing press, and the other equipment that belonged to the Palestinian newspaper *Filastin*, produced in Jaffa before 1948 until a few weeks before the city was occupied by Israeli forces. Mustafa Kabha, 'al-Sihafa al-Arabiyya fi Zil al-Hukm al-'Askari', in Mustafa Kabha (ed.), *al-Aqaliyya al-Arabiyya al-Filastiniyya fi Israel*, (Haifa: Mada al-Karmil, 2014), 130-139.

10 Mustafa Kabha, *al-Aqaliyya*, 151-153.

11 The Palestinian Communist party was first established in 1919; this party merged with the Israeli Communist Party in 1948 by the name Makai under Arab and Jewish leadership. The Arab and some Jewish membership split from this party in 1956 on ideological grounds, and formed the Palestinian Communist Party, Rakah.

12 Mustafa Kabha, *al-Aqaliyya*, 123-170. Other papers were also issued by individuals, or Israeli state agencies. Many Arabic-speaking Jewish immigrants from Arab countries were instrumental in the production of Arabic-medium newspapers and journals. For example, *al-Yawm* [Today], issued by Michael Assaf in Jaffa in 1948; Assaf was a managing member of the Hebrew newspaper Davar, which was an official organ of the Israeli government; *Haqiqat al-'Amr*, a weekly paper (1949-1969) connected with the Israeli General Guild of Workers, the Histadrut; The Leftist Labor Mapai issued the weekly *al-Mirsad*.

13 Hanna Abu Hanna (d. February 2, 2022), *Rihlat al-Bahth 'an al-Turath*, (Haif: al-Wadi al-Akhdar, 1994), 109; Habeeb Qahwaji, *al-Arab fi Zil al-*

Ihtilal al-Israeli Munzu 1948, (Beirut: Markiz al-Abhath, 1972), 281-300.

14 A poetry festival was initiated by Michel Haddad (1919-1997) at the YMCA in Nazareth on March 12, 1955. This festival did not address national or political issues; most of the poems were lyrics about love and romance, description, philosophical notions. Few poems dealt with societal issues, for example poverty, unemployment. The sixteen poets attending this festival decided to establish the Rabitat Shu'ara' al-Arabiyya, "Arab Poets Organization." Haddad founded and edited a journal by the name *al-Mujtama'*, "The Society".

15 See Hanna Abu Hanna, *Rihlat al-Bahth*, 110-111; *al-Jadid*, 16th year), Issue 3, (March 1969), 26; Habeeb Qahwaji, *Al-Arab fi Zil*), 286.

16 Mahmoud Darwish credits Hanna Abu Hanna, a poet, essayist and teacher, for pioneering the introduction of free verse in Palestine/Israel in one of the public poetry *mahrajans*. Poems translated in this work were written in free verse, the prevalent style in modern Arabic poetry. For further information, see Hanna Abu Hanna, *Rihlat al-Bahth*, 111, and *al-Jadid,* 16th year, Issue 3 (March, 1969), 26.

17 Such statements were written by these poets in introductions of their anthologies, cited in Shmuel Moreh, *Bibliography of Arabic Books and Periodicals Published in Israel 1948-1972.* (Jerusalem: Mount Scopus Center, 1974.)

18 The state formed with the name of the United Arabic Republic resulted from the merger of Egypt and Syria in February 1958. This union was viewed by many as a first step in unifying Arab countries. This union, however, lasted only three years, 1958-1961. The royal family in Iraq was viewed as a collaborator, especially with the British, who promised Palestine as a Jewish homeland in what has come to be known as the Balfour Declaration in November 1917. Palestinians see this as the source of the loss of their country in 1948.

19 The Palestinian poet Tawfiq Zayyad advocated collecting Palestinian folkloric songs and *zajal* before they were lost. To that end, he published a book titled *'an al-'Adab wa al-'Adab al-Sha'bi fi Filastin* (On Literature and Folklore literature in Palestine) in 1970. A sample of works on Palestinian folk poetry includes the following: Nadia G. Yaqub, *Pens, Swords and the Springs of Art: the Oral Poetry Dueling of Palestinian Weddings in the Galilee* (Amsterdam: Brill, 2006); Dirgham Hanna Sbait, *The Improvised-sung Folk*

Introduction

Poetry of the Palestinians (Washington: University of Washington, 1982); Saud Asadi, *Aghani min al-Jalil: 'ash'ar Zajaliyya* (Nazereth: Matba'at al-Hakim, 1976); Nimr Sirhan, *Mawsu'at al-folklore al-Filastini* (Beirut: Munzamat al-Tahrir al-Filastiniyya, 1989); Musa Hafiz, *Funun al-Zajal al-sha'bi al-Filastini* (Jerusalem: Manshurat al-Bayadir, 1988).

20 See, for example, Raja al-Naqqash, *Mahmoud Darwish Sha'ir al-Arad al-Muhtalla*, 2nd ed. (Cairo: Dar al-Hilal, 1971); Abbas, Khidr, Adab al-Muqawama (Cairo: Dar al-Katib al-Arabi, 1968).

The poet Salem Jubran states in an interview by Riyadh Baydas that Palestinians in Israel had only two choices: either ally yourself with the Israeli authorities and gain personal privileges such as work or be prepared to stand up and struggle for the rights of your people against the oppression of the government. See *al-Jadid*, Vol. 37, Issue 1 (January 1988), 26-31.

21 Further works dealing with this topic include Ghali Shukri, *Adab al-Muqawama*, (Cairo: Dar al-Ma'arif, 1970); Adonis's *Zaman al-Shi'r*, (Beirut, Dar al-Saqi, 2005), especially the articles 'Hawla al-shi'r wa al-thawra,' "on poetry and revolution," and 'Istitradat hawla al-shi'r wa al-thawra,' "excursuses (Detailed Discussions) on poetry and revolution," 205-228, and 229-249, respectively.

22 Adonis, 'al-Kitaba al-Ibda'iyya wa al-Kitaba al-Wazifiyya' "Creative Writing and Functional Writing," in *Zaman al-Shi'r*, 199 ff.

23 Shmuel Moreh, *Bibliography of Arabic Books and Periodicals Published in Israel 1948-1972* (Jerusalem: Mount Scopus Center, 1974), 12-13.

24 Mahmoud Darwish, *Shay''an al-Watan*, (Beirut: Dar al-Awda. n.d.), 317-323.

25 Translation mine. See *Zaman al-Shi'r*, 222-223.

27

POETS and POEMS

Asma Rizq Toubi
(1905–1983)

TO JAFFA

With the open road
hearts fluttered.
They ran with their emotions
oppressed by the hand of diaspora
over twenty years.

They rushed with their yearning,
a love deeply weathered by torment
to search for their homes
so they could kiss their doorsteps,
kiss that earth.

She proceeded to those homes,
those precious homes!
She rushed to Jaffa alight with
nostalgic memories,
and from walkway to walkway
wishing to . . . ?
Wishing for what . . . ?

In front of the door of her beloved house,
she stood stone-still.
Would she knock on its door?
What would she say to its inhabitants?

Would she retrace her steps in vain?
Certainly not! She would knock and express
her sacred resentment,
a blazing flame!
She knocked. The stranger answered,
and proceeded to ask: "What do you want?
And who do you want to see?"
With her head held high she said:
"Do you not know this is my house?
That bed is my nuptial bed,
that wardrobe is mine, my children's.
Don't you know what you have done?"
With docility, acquired by old age,
she responded with evasions:
"I bought it and paid money,
I paid in cash . . . Trust me!"
The other replied with the pride of expectation
in a great future:
"It was mine and you took it,
it will come back to me,
I am fully certain.
The deeds of oppressors never endure!
Oppression is the breeding ground for disaster."

1972

Fadwa Tuqan
(1917–2003)

THE PLAGUE

The day the plague spread through my city
I rushed out into the wilderness
with arms open to the sky
entreating the winds from the depths of sorrow:
"Oh winds blow and drive the clouds towards us,
bring down the rain
to cleanse the air in my city,
to cleanse houses, hills and trees!
Oh, winds, blow and drive the clouds towards us.
Let the rain descend!
Let the rain descend!
Let it descend."

c. 1989

Fadwa Tuqan

A LETTER TO TWO CHILDREN
ON THE EAST BANK OF JORDAN
For Karma and Omar

Oh my Karma, I wish I could fly
on the wings of love, I wish I could!
But my longing, oh, my little one, is shackled, a prisoner!
The crossing is not possible, my little Karma!
The River[1] separates the road between us;
here they are stationed.
Like a black curse, they are stationed here.
They have blown up, blown up the bridges
and deprived me of you, my little one –
and they forbade the crossing.

Death lurks on the River.
Death awaits whoever crosses.
Oh my Karma, my precious gazelle,
the clear shining honey of your eyes –
I miss them sorely
and the blond locks of hair like wheat,
like the harvest season in our fields
I miss them, I miss them sorely.
I wish I could fly to you, my precious gazelle!

c. 1988
1 Reference to the River Jordan between Palestine/Israel and Jordan.

35

HAMZA

– 1 –

Hamza was
one like others from my town
kind, earning his bread
through the dint of toil like decent, simple folk.

He said to me one day when we met
as I was knocking around in the vast wasteland of defeat:
"Hold on, do not lose heart, my cousin.
This land razed
by the fire of crime,
withering today in sadness and silence –
this land will keep
its betrayed heart alive, never dying.

This land is a woman
in its furrows and wombs.
The mystery of fertility is the same:
the force that grows palm trees
and ears of grain
grows a fighting people."

Days went by when I did not see
my cousin

but I was aware
that the land panted and trembled
with labor and a new birth.

– 2 –

Sixty-five years became
a massive boulder breaking his back
when the governor of the town issued the order:
"Blow up the house and tie up
his son in the torture chamber."
Then he stood up
to sing the praises of love and security
and peace building.

The soldiers cordoned the grounds of the house.
The snake coiled
and efficiently carried out
the completion of the deadly circle.
Loud commands blasted:
"Leave the house!" And they granted generously
an hour or so.

Hamza opened the balconies
to the sun under the eyes of the soldiers,
then cried "Allahu Akbar"
and called out:
"Oh, Palestine, know today
I, the house and my children are sacrifices for your
   redemption.

For you we live and die."
A quiver spread along the nerves of the town
when the echo repeated Hamza's cry,
then silence and submission enveloped the house.

One hour
and the façade of the martyred house
heaved and collapsed.
The debris of the rooms twisted
to embrace the dreams, the warmth that once was
enveloping the harvest of a lifetime,
the memory of years,
built with hard work, persistence, grief
and happy laughter.

Yesterday I saw my cousin on the road
winding his way along the path, determined and sure.
Hamza was still holding his head high.

1969

Fadwa Tuqan

AT ALLENBY BRIDGE

*"From the Images of the Zionist Occupation: Sighs in Front of the
Official Crossing-Permits Window"*

The wait at the Bridge, begging to cross—
yes, begging to cross.
My asphyxia, my short breath wafted out ablaze
at noontime.
Seven hours of waiting!
What clipped the wings of time,
who crippled the noon?
The summer heat scourges my brows,
sweat drips salt into my eyes.
Yes, thousands of eyes
whose fervent desire suspends mirrors of pain
over the window of Official Permits, models
of anticipation and patience.
Yes, we are begging to cross.
Then the voice of a vicious soldier booms
like a blow falling on the face of the crowd:
"Arabs! Chaos! You dogs!
Go back, do not approach the barrier, go back, you dogs!"
Then a hand slams shut the permits window
blocking the road in the face of the crowd.
Yes, my humanness bleeds, my heart

39

drips rancor, my blood is poison and fire.
"Arabs! Chaos! You dogs . . ."
Ah, where are you Mu'tasim?[1]
Ah, for the tribal revenge!
All I possess today is waiting around . . .
What clipped the wings of time?
Who crippled the noon?
The summer heat scourges my brows,
sweat drips salt into my eyes.
Ah, my wounds!
That scourge scrubbed my wound with landmines
if only one could see . . .
Oh, the humiliation of the captive!
Bitter I became, my taste murderous
my hatred is fearsome, bottomless,
my heart is stone, sulfuric, a fountain of fire
a thousand Hend under my skin,[2]
the hunger of my hatred
its mouth agape, nothing but their livers
satisfies the hunger taking root in my body.
Oh, this fearsome, kindled hatred,
they killed love in the depth of my heart.
They turned the blood in my veins
into pus and tar.

c. 1993

---

1 Mu'tasim, the notable Abbasid Caliph (ruled 833–842), fought against the
   Byzantine Empire. Upon learning that an Arab woman kidnapped by the
   Byzantine army invoked his name to rescue her with the phrase, "Where

are you, Mu'tasim?" he personally led the celebrated Sack of Amorium, free-
ing the woman. Her call became symbolic of help in moments of crisis.

2 Hend bint Utba belonged to the Quraysh tribe of Muhammad, and her fam-
ily at first strongly opposed the new religion. In the battle of Badr (624 A.D.),
which Muhammad waged against the Meccans, Hend's father was killed by
Hamza, a cousin of Muhammad; her brother also fell. A year later, Hamza
died in the battle of Uhud against the non-Muslim Meccans. Legend has it
that Hend wanted to avenge the Meccans killed in the battle of Badr, espe-
cially her father and brother, by splitting Hamza's body and chewing his
liver. She subsequently acquired the epithet Hend, the liver-eater; her
heinous act symbolizes the maximum desire for vengeance.

I SHALL NEVER CRY

*To the poets of the resistance in the Occupied
Territories for the last twenty years. A gift for
our gathering in Haifa, March 4, 1968.*

At the gates of Jaffa, oh, my loved ones,
in the disarray of destroyed homes
between thorns and rubble,
I stood and addressed my eyes: "Oh, eyes:
stop and let us weep
for the ruins of those who departed and left this behind."
The house calls out for those who built it,
each wall a eulogy for those who built it.
The heart, crushed, choked,

the heart asked: "What did
time do to you, oh house?
And where are the inhabitants?
Did you, after separation, did you
receive any news?
Here they were!
Here they dreamed!
Here they drew
plans for the near future.
Where are the inhabitants, the dreams, and the future?
Where are they?"
The ruins of the house did not speak.
Nothing spoke except their absence,
the silence of silence, and abandonment;
and there was a group of owls and specters
alien in face, hand, and tongue
circling around the edges
setting down roots in the soil.
They were the absolute masters,
and they were . . . and they were.
My heart choked with sorrow.

Beloved ones,
I wiped the grey fog of tears from my eyes
so to meet you with eyes alight with love and faith
in you, the land, and humanity.
How shameful had I come to meet you
with eyes wet, blinking
and with a despairing, defeated heart!
And here I am, my loved ones, among you

to borrow an ember from you
to take, oh lanterns in the dark,
a drop of your oil
for my own lantern.
And here I am, my loved ones.
I extend my hand to yours
and by your heads I rest my head,
and with you lift my face to the sun.
Here you are as strong as the rocks of our mountains,
like the flowers of our sweet countryside.
So, how could the wound crush me?
How could despair crush me?
How could I cry in front of you?
Upon my word, I shall not cry hereafter!
My loved ones, the horse of the people has overcome
yesterday's stumble,
the noble one has awoken beyond the river.
Look! The horse of the people
is neighing, sure of its desire,
escaping the siege of calamity and gloom,
galloping toward its port in the sun.
There gather throngs of knights
to bless, to redeem him
from the water of the ravine,
and from the blood of corals
they provide him drink;
they give him in great abundance
fodder from their bodies.
And they cheer the unfettered horse:
gallop on, oh, you

horse of the people!
You, the symbol and the sign,
and we, a battalion, stand behind you!
Our seething and surging will never abate,
nor anger
nor in the battlefield shall exhaustion
appear on our faces
nor will we rest
until we banish the specters
and the ravens and the darkness.

My loved ones, lanterns in the dark, my brothers
in the wound.
Oh, you, the secret of yeast, the wheat germ
dying here to give us,
give us,
give us.
In your footsteps I will follow
and plant, like you, my feet in my homeland –
in my land
and fix, like you, my eyes
on the path of splendor and the sun.

MY SORROWFUL CITY ON THE DAY OF THE ZIONIST OCCUPATION

The day we saw death and betrayal
the tide withdrew,
the opening in the skylight shut,
the city held its breath.
The day the waves collapsed,
the marshlands surrendered their face to the light,
hope turned into ashes.
And my sorrowful city choked on the lump of affliction.

The children and songs vanished.
There was neither shadow nor echo.
The sorrow in my city crept nakedly
with blood-stained steps.
Silence fell over my city.
The silence was entrenched like mountains,
like the night it was; the silence was excruciating,
loaded
with the weight of death and defeat.
Oh, my silent, sorrowful city!
Is it so that at harvest time
crops and fruit burn down into ashes?
Oh, what an end!
Oh, what an end!

c. 1967

Mu'in Bseiso
(1926–1984)

THE GOD OF JERUSALEM

May my right-hand forget me,
may the eyes of my beloved forget me,
may my brother forget me,
may my only friend forget me,
may slumber forget me
on a bed of sleeplessness,
just as a weapon
in the height of battle
forgets the hand of the warrior,
and as a watchman
forgets about the foxes in his vineyards,
if I forget
that in the heart of our land lives
the god of Jerusalem,
and that from the harvest
of our blood he extracts
milk and honey
and vintage wine
so that he lives
and slaughters beasts
so that I build
from tears
a wailing-wall, and turn
my tent into a handkerchief

to lament
our diaspora
with no hope of return.

May my right hand forget me,
may the lilting eyes of my people forget me,
if I forget
to thrust into the road that leads
to the bosom of our orange orchards and vineyards
the sword of hell
in the eyes of the god of Jerusalem.

1979

Harun Hashim Rasheed
(1926–1984)

AMONG STRANGERS[1]

Laila came to her father
with pain in her eyes,
and fire in her gut
ablaze with yearning.
Her eyes were clouded
with visions weakened by sickness.
Bureij[2] has put sorrow to sleep,
so there is neither voice nor tune.
Laila came to her father
when the years had weighed him down.
She said in a state of urgency,
parched with pain:
"Why, Father,
are we,
why are we strangers?
Don't we have
friends and loved ones in this world?
Don't we have intimate friends?
Don't we have dear ones?
Why, Father,
are we . . . ?
Why are we strangers?
Why are we strangers?
Year follows year,

Father, without change,
no hope, no good news,
only pain and sorrow,
only sadness and affliction,
only a voice of fate
always hailing
my homeland.
Why?
Are we, Father
why, Father, are we strangers?

Why
are we suffering,
in dejection and poverty,
continuing to wander
from one country to another?
Did we not have land,
where hopes flourished?
Where good news danced
above and birds sang?
Did we not have a homeland
whose name time glorified?
Why?
Are we, Father . . .
Why are we strangers?

Doesn't
our verdant land,
with its fresh water springs,
and sweet dreams

radiate with love?
Why do we no longer till
as free people with our own hands
and harvest the fruit of our country
to give and receive?
Why do we not
furnish it
with hard work so it nourishes us?
Why?
Are we, Father?
Why are we strangers?

Why are we in tents
in heat and cold?
Can we not go back home
and to the fields and to dignity?
Why are we in pain,
in hunger and in sickness
in misery and in affliction?
Why?
Are we, Father?
Why are we strangers?

I asked you
yesterday about my mother,
who left and did not return.
I asked,
my heart beating in anguish.
I asked, tears in my eyes
and you, immersed in silence,

neither speak nor hear.
Your silence is vehement, Father.
Your voice does not rescue me
so I shout:
Father, tell me
why are we strangers?

I asked you
a few days ago,
I asked you about my brother Ahmad.
You were about to remove from my sight
that black thought,
you were about to say: he died,
oh, Laila, he was martyred,
but you did not!
Why didn't you do so?
Why?
Are we Father?
Why are we strangers?

Do you remember Salwa, Father?
I saw her yesterday,
troubled in the alleyway, lost, homeless,
sad, miserable.
Sickness has changed her
over time, oh Father,
it was not her, certainly
this is not my friend,
eyes full of pain
and a body all diseased.

Why?
Are we, Father?
Why are we strangers?

Father!
Please, by God, tell me
will we ever go to Jaffa?
Its cherished image
has been floating before my eyes.
Will we ever enter it with pride,
despite the times, in dignity?
Will I enter my room, tell me?
Will I enter it with my dreams?
And will I meet it, and it me?
Will it hear my footsteps?
Will I enter it by way of this heart
so homesick, thirsty?
Father,
had I, like birds,
wings to carry me,
I'd have flown in a heedless longing
out of yearning for my country.
But I am of the earth;
the earth continues to bind me."

A hot tear
quivers,
it flows, and after,
another.
His daughter's cry thunders

hammering his ears in the gloom,
and he shouts: "We shall regain it,
we shall regain that country,
never shall we accept a substitute for it,
never shall we accept a price for it!

No hunger will kill us,
no poverty will burden us,
hope will prevail
whenever vengeance beckons.
Patience, my daughter, patience.
Tomorrow, victory will be on our side."

Gaza, 1951

1 This poem appeared in an anthology entitled *Ma' al-Ghuraba'* [Among
   Strangers] published in Cairo in 1954. The Lebanese Diva Fayrouz sang
   it in 1955, with musical composition by her husband 'Asi al-Rahhbani
   and brother-in-law Mansur.
2 Bureij: A Palestinian refugee camp in the Central Gaza Strip, established
   in 1949 after the expulsion of Palestinians from their homeland.

Tawfiq Zayyad
(1929–1994)

A NATION ON THE CROSS

They hung us, the whole nation, on the cross,
they crucified us
to repent.
This setback is not
the end of the world,
nor are we slaves.

Wipe your tears,
bury the dead,
rise up again.

Oh, you sorrowful people,
you are the world,
and the only source of grace.
You are the history
and a bright future
in this life.

Come,
let us join hands,
walk into the fire.
The future of the free, no matter how distant,
no matter how distant,
is near.

DARE

The earth does not drink my blood,
nor does my soul relent.
Kill me . . . I dare you,
crucify me . . . I dare you,
steal my morsel of bread . . . I dare you,
destroy my house, leave it in ruins,
I dare you
eat me, drink me, I dare you.

My home, I offer myself in sacrifice.
You are my hopes, dripping honey,
you are the ordeal and the love
that consumes my life
the love and light of my eyes,
the love that fills my being.

This land is my homeland.
her skies are my infatuation,
my present, future, my cradle and place of death,
my blood, my flesh, my heart and ribs,
my mother, father,
my children, grandparents,
my heritage, songs, banners, and glory,
my lofty home and quest.

I am the sad people,
the tortured people,
the wild violent storm,
in the face of injustice.
I am the river that runs, and runs,
drowning all oppressors;
I am a volcano of love for my homeland,
I am the vegetation, the sun
and drops of dew.
Kill me, I dare you,
crucify me, I dare you,
the earth does not drink my blood
nor will my soul relent.

1985

HERE WE ARE STAYING

As if we were twenty impossibilities
in Lod, Ramla and Galilee![1]
Here we are, staying like a wall on your chests,
in your throats
like a piece of glass, like prickly pear thorns
in your eyes,
a firestorm.
Here we are, staying like a wall on your chests
cleaning dishes in bars,
refilling glasses for the masters,
polishing tiles in sooty kitchens
to snatch a morsel for our young
from your blue teeth.
Here we are, staying like a wall on your chests.
We experience hunger,
nakedness,
we challenge,
sing poetry,
and fill the angry streets with demonstrations,
fill the prisons with pride,
make babies . . . rebellious generation
after rebellious generation
as if we were twenty impossibilities
in Lod, Ramla and Galilee.

Here we are staying!
Go and drink the sea!
We guard the shade of fig trees and olives,
grow ideas like yeast in dough,
with the chill of ice in our veins.
In our hearts burns a blazing hellfire.
If we are thirsty we will squeeze the rocks,
will eat dirt if hungry,
but we will never leave.
With our sweet blood
we are generous,
we are generous,
we are generous.
Here, we have a past,
a present,
and a future.
As if we were twenty impossibilities
in Lod, Ramla and Galilee
may our living root stay firm
and strike deep in the soil.

Better for the oppressor to review his account
before the tables are turned.
And every action . . . Please read
what comes in the Holy Book.

1965

1 Lod and Ramla are two cities in central Palestine/Israel.

I FIRMLY CLASP YOUR HANDS

I call out to you, my people,
I firmly clasp your hands,
I kiss the earth beneath your feet
and declare: I sacrifice myself for you.
I give you the light of my eyes as a gift,
I give you the warmth of my heart.
The tragedy I live
is my share of your own.

I call upon you,
I firmly clasp your hands.
In my land I never was disgraced,
never lowered myself.
I always challenged my oppressors,
orphaned, naked and with bare feet.
I felt my blood in my own hands,
never lowered my flag.
I always protected the grass
on my ancestors' graves.

I call out to you, my people,
I firmly clasp your hands.

1966

LEAVE US ALONE

Leave our people alone,
do not throw more wood into the fire.
How can you live on board a ship
and provoke an ocean of flames?
Leave our people alone,
You deaf ones who have stuffed
your ears with cotton and mud.
For the thousandth time we tell you:
We do not eat the flesh of others
we do not kill children, nor
do we kill peaceful people;
We do not loot houses,
nor the produce of the field,
nor do we blind eyes;
we do not steal antiquities,
we do not know the taste of crime,
we do not burn books,
nor do we break pens;
we do not blackmail the weak.
Leave our people alone.
You deaf ones, who have stuffed
your ears with cotton and mud.
For the thousandth time we tell you:
I swear by the sun

of this free soil we will not
lose a speck!
We will never bend
to fire and weapons,
not even by a hair's breadth.

                                        1969

LET THE WHOLE WORLD HEAR

Let the whole world hear,
let it hear!
We shall go hungry, naked
we shall be torn to pieces
we shall eat your earth,
oh, land deep in suffering!
We shall face death, but
shall never abandon
the unfurled flag of the free.
We shall never succumb
to brutal force, to Phantom jets, to cannons.
Never shall a single one of us surrender,
never shall one of us surrender
not even one suckling babe.

1969

Youssef al-Khatib
(1931–2011)

THE LARK

There, my friend, is a lark
at the border
who has violated a thousand sacred
prohibitions.
She flits here and there, free,
while I am weighed down with my wounds.
I wish I were a lark
in flight
with beating wings
in the air
over our orange orchard
and pond.
I wish I were a lark.

1955

Rashid Hussein
(1936–1977)

Rashid Hussein

LOVE AND THE GHETTO[1]

Jaffa, My City

Chimneys of hashish dispense torpor in Jaffa,
its barren roads pregnant with flies and grief.
Jaffa's heart is silent, bolted by a stone.
Sama Street holds a funeral cortège for the moon.

Jaffa is without a heart, then?
Jaffa is without a moon?
Jaffa is blood on stone?
Jaffa, from whose breasts I suckled the milk of oranges,
is parched? Jaffa, who supplied the rain from her waves!
Jaffa, from whose breasts I suckled the milk of oranges,
her arm paralyzed,
her back broken!
Jaffa, the orchard whose trees were men,
now felled into a hash den dispensing torpor!

Those ignorant of Jaffa
have not heard how she rose in blossoms.
They have not heard Jaffa was a city
whose trade consisted of oranges.
One day she was destroyed: they turned
her trade into the export of refugees

1965

69

THE WOMAN AND THE LAND

He sold his land to the Zionists to pay for his fiancée's dowry.

She wrote in response:

You sold our sacred soil, you basest of lovers
to pay for my dowry,
and to buy me a fancy wedding dress?
So, what would I tell your child if he were to ask?
"Do I have a homeland?"
What would I tell him if he inquired?
"YOU are the cost?"
You pulled the gardens from her hair,
sold the tresses of her olive trees,
debased the honor of her farmland at the *souk*,[2]
betrayed her faithful orchards,
cut the nipples of her lemons,
and sold the tresses of her olive trees!

****

Would you betray the mother who nursed you to betroth me
and starve these threshing floors
so that my womb might be sated?

Would you make a nuptial feast for my grieving heart
from the blight of our country?
Would the nakedness of the threshing floors, base husband,
clothe me with jasmine?

c. 1958

1 This is an abridged poem from a longer one, first published in
   al-Jadid, Issue No. 1, 1965.
2 *souk*: marketplace

Abdel Wahab Zahida
(1939–2010)

THE IDENTITY DOCUMENTS
OF FATHER CHRISTMAS

Do not ask
what we can do.
Tonight
Father Christmas
may not arrive.

He may come; that is possible.
He may not come; that is also possible.
The roads to the Church of the Nativity are barricaded.
The sighs of orphans, the prayers of the elderly
are cannons of woe
bombarding even Father Christmas.
On this night
the beast is ready near the Manger.
He devours the infant with no remorse.
Do not ask . . .

Even if he came, he would lose his way.
He will not find happiness among the people.
He will not find anything but frost.
They sawed down the palm trees . . . discussion ended,
crucified the babe while suckling,

killed al–Durra,[1]
bombarded the Manger,[2]
trampled over the Dome of the Rock,[3]
demolished the Temple.[4]
The cup has overflowed.
How could Father Christmas come
while the Nativity is in shackles?
Do not ask . . .

He will come . . . for sure he will come!
In another year he will arrive
and enter through all the doors,
through the Lions' Gate[5]
through the Golden Gate[6]
through the Coptic Monastery
through the Najma Suq.[7]
He does not fear the darkness,
silencers or rubber bullets.
He will come . . . He will come
through Khan Al–Zayt,[8]
through the door of the house.
So, do not cry.
Listen!
The horses' hooves
will trample despair
while candles
illuminate the night,
and Father Christmas comes
bearing gifts like a river
and carrying the *mahmal.*[9]

Bear with it,
adorn yourself with patience,
bear with it.
Tomorrow is more beautiful and lovely.
Should the Lord not ask after us,
who else should He ask after?

c. 2007

1 Mohammad al-Durra, a twelve-year old, was killed in Gaza by Israeli soldiers while seeking cover from a crossfire during the Second Intifada in 2000.
2 The Manger in the Church of the Nativity in Bethlehem.
3 The famous golden Islamic edifice in Jerusalem.
4 The Western Wall.
5 *Bab al-Asbat* in Arabic, a gate in the Jerusalem Ottoman Wall.
6 *Bab al-Rahma* in Arabic, a gate in the Jerusalem Ottoman Wall.
7 A market in Jerusalem.
8 *khan*: an inn for travelers built around a courtyard. *Khan al-Zayt* is such a place in Old Jerusalem.
9 *mahmal*: the ceremonial palanquin made of embroidered fabrics, was a symbol of the sultan's authority, traditionally carried on a camel with the pilgrim caravan from Cairo to Mecca.

Samih al-Qasim
(1939–2014)

Samih al-Qasim

A LETTER FROM JAIL

I had neither paper nor pen
and from the intense heat and bitterness of pain,
my dear friends, I could not sleep.
Thus, I thought: what if I while away the time with poetry?
Meanwhile, I had a visitor through the hole of the black cell.
Please do not make fun of me. Yes, a bat came to visit me!
He started with full vigor
to peck at the walls in my black cell.
I called out: "Hey, brave visitor,
tell me, don't you have news from our world?
For a long time, sir, I have not
read newspapers here, nor heard the news.
Tell me about the world, family, my loved ones!"
But he, without answers,
flapped his black wings through my cell and flew away.
I called out: "Hey, strange visitor,
relax! Won't you carry my news to friends?"

From the intensity of the heat, bedbugs, pain,
my dear friends, I could not sleep!
The poor guard was still behind the door
still shuffling his feet in boredom,
like me unable to sleep,
like me, without a reason, jailed.

77

I leaned my back against the wall
shattered, like a dove in a bottomless whirlpool,
my brain burning.
Oh, mother, how sad I am
that for my sake your nights are torture
crying silently, expecting the return
of my beloved brothers from work,
unable to eat,
and my chair is empty. No laughter, no talk.
Oh, mother, how painful
that you burst out in tears
when friends ask you about me.
But, oh, mother, I believe,
I believe that the beauty of life
is born in prison,
and that my last visitor will never be
a bat entering blindly.
Daylight will surely be my visitor,
And the jailer, surprised, will bow!
And my jail will collapse, yes, collapse
shattered, aflame by daylight.

c. 1959–1964

THE GATE OF TEARS

Our loved ones across the border
anxiously, painfully await our return,
their arms are wide open to hold us, feel us,
their hearts are crucibles of pain
beating in inaudible lament!
Their eyes bewildered; their lips quivering
with questions about the home of our ancestors
drowned in tears of pain, degradation, and regret.

Our loved ones across the border
await a grain of their wheat.
How goes our deserted home?
How goes the face of the land?
Will it recognize us when we return?
Have pity on us,
remnants of an expelled, wandering people.
Oh, have pity on us, living the life of slaves.
Will we ever return? Will we ever return?

c. 1959–1964

Salem Jubran
(1941–2011)

1948

-1-

The black night of *The Nakba*[1] had no rays of light
except the flashes of bombs
striking villages not at war.
Why so, my homeland?
Our eyes spoke in horror,
failing to see all there was to see.
With anxiety ablaze they said:
we cast glass marbles onto the wretched ground
and returned to our homes.

-2-

Why so, Father?
Would you say that Lebanon is as beautiful as our homeland,
would you say that it has beautiful garden plots,
where childhood dreams might find contentment?
Would you say it has young children, as in our country, oh
    Father?
Would you say it has food?
Not a word!
My father's eyes brimmed with tears for the first time.
He was like steel, all his life.

Tears in the eye of the free are embers of live coals.
The ceiling wood beams were snakes, the wall
was startled, the weather was dizzying.
This house, Mother
was never precious;
so why has it now become so cherished and so beautiful,
    I wonder?
O sweet water, ever generous
all these years,
who will drink you after today, I wonder,
who will it be, sorrowful spring?

–3–

Hush!
A voice is calling out.
Who could it be?
For God's sake, listen for a moment!
It is the sorrowful voice of Abu Radhi:
"Hey, Eisa, get over here,
leave the water . . . leave the shovel,
leave everything and get over here."
A thousand voices came rising from the rooftops
rumbling, strangled, wounded:
"O shepherd behind the *tal*[2]
leave the flocks wherever they are;
if sheep are lost, would you say that is a tragedy
when all the people in the land are lost?
O farmer,
clearing the brush is no use.

82

On the horizon there is loss,
on the horizon there is dispersal,
this year the land will lie fallow
and so will it remain for a thousand years,
leave your hoe,
let us keep it as a living memorial to the people
to remain among the hills,
come join me!"
Hush! . . . a terrifying voice.

-4-

Who could it be?
Get to the window, Khazna, and look!
"Oh, my God, how awful, how awful!"
My mother shouted in horror,
stirring our blood to the fullest.
We all rushed over the wall.
Surely Suhmata[3] was a fire of hell,
where life was incinerated.
Comrades
and friends from the village of Suhmata,
I have never forgotten, though I was young,
the fate to which we were heading.

1964

1 *Nakba*: The Arabic word for the fall of Palestine to the Israelis in 1948
   and the catastrophe that befell the Palestinians.
2 *tal* or *tel*: A small hill.
3 Suhmata: A Palestinian village in Northern Galilee whose citizens
   were forced into exile by the Israelis in October 1948.

A HANGED MAN

*"A toy for children was made available for sale
in the Israeli markets depicting a hanged Arab."*

A hanged man,
the sweetest toy.
The sweetest entertainment for kids
is available in the *souk*.[1]
It is no longer in the *souk,*
it is sold out. It ran out many days ago.
Do not search for it; let your child understand,
it ran out days ago.

Oh, souls of the dead
in the Nazi concentration camps,
the hanged man
is not a Jew in Berlin;
the hanged man
is an Arab, like me, of my people
hanged by your brethren.
Pardon me . . . hanged by Nazis – like
those in Zion.

Oh, souls of the dead
in the Nazi concentration camps,
if only you knew! . . . If only you knew . . .

1964

1 *souk*: marketplace

A REFUGEE

The sun crosses borders
without soldiers firing shots
at its face.
In the morning, the nightingale chirps
into Tulkarm.[1]
In the evening,
he eats dinner and goes to sleep
safely,
with the birds of the Jewish kibbutzim.[2]
A lost donkey
grazing in no-man's land,
grazing safely
without soldiers firing shots
at its face.
And I . . . your refugee
Oh, land of my homeland!
The border walls block
my eyes and your horizon.

1965

1 Tulkarm: A city on the West Bank, Northern Palestine.
2 kibbutz (pl. kibbutzim): A utopian agricultural collective community
   established by Zionists in Palestine.

Salem Jubran

A SONG[1]

Like oak trees here we shall stay,
like boulders,
like beautiful olive trees on the hilltops of my country,
like streams.
Like pigeons in the green valley
we will flap our wings over your soil,
Oh, my homeland,
like eagles.

Had it not been for you, would we have been but corpses?
Had it not been for us, would you have been but graves?
Like oak trees
here we shall stay,
like boulders.
I shall remain on your slaughtered soil, my homeland,
flute in hand, singing for springtime,

saying to those tearful and despairing ones:
winter will surely die: smile,
do not lose heart under your tears
give me your hands, the battle for survival needs you
soldiers . . . as does the quest for our return.

Death to the mercenary newcomer and the coward,
and glory to the people who endure
and still walk over thorns
to birth spring.

1964

1 This poem was titled "Qasidtan 'an al-Watan" ("Two Poems about
Homeland") in Yusuf al-Khatib's *Diwan al-Watan al-Muhtull* [Poetry
Anthology from the Occupied Homeland]. In S. Jubran's original an-
thology *Kalimat min al-Qalb* [Words from the heart], published in
Akka (Acre) (n.d.) and in his *al-'A'mal al-Shi'riyya al-Ka*mila [Com-
plete Poetical Works] published in Haifa 2012, the title of this poem
was given as "Ughnia" ("A Song.") There are also differences of word-
ing in al-Khatib's version. However, the translation of the poem is
based on the version in Jubran's original anthology and his *Complete
Works*.

EVENING STROLL

My mother is sick and has no medicine.
Her cries grieve in solitude.
No one hears her call.
She looks up to the sky in hope
and it spits in her doleful face . . . how miserly it is!
How miserly the sky!
And my brothers . . .
God, how wonderful you are, my young brothers.
The fullness of spring is in your eyes,
but the claws of winter have assailed,
have shredded it savagely.
Your eyes, I see them, beg me for a gift;
they want something . . . a toy . . . oranges . . .
They want me to keep my promise, to come to you
on the Eve of Eid with a pair of shoes.[1]

My mother, my brothers, and a thousand stories
are on my mind; they pain me,
exhaust my nerves, fail to leave me,
immolate me.
And you, my friend, with those innocent eyes, ask me
for a glass of cognac in the evening.

Of course, at my expense –
from the price of medicine,
from the price of shoes.
What would my mother say
if she knew?
What would my brothers say?
Excuse me, please. I am exhausted, my friend,
I shall not go for a stroll . . . this evening.

1964

1 Eid: A communal religious or national celebration, such as Independence Day or Christmas, at the end of the month of Ramadan.

Salem Jubran

IN LIEU OF AN ELEGY

He was tall, my neighbor,
and handsome like a palm tree.
His laughter was clear,
pure like jasmine.
At the end of an eight-hour shift at Nu'man's,
he
used to return home, eat, wash up,
and play with Etan . . .
on a wooden horse.
For hours he used to play with Etan.

A week ago
my neighbor didn't go to work at Nu'man's,
he didn't return home to eat, wash up,
and play with Etan.
A week ago,
the black notice in our quarter[1]
announced another downpour of blood
that drenched the thirsty desert sands.
On display: the death of a man.

                                        1970

---

1 Customarily, printed flyers in black ink giving the name of the
  deceased and information about their family and life function as death
  notices. The flyers are often posted in public places.

91

KUFR QASIM[1]

The blood hasn't dried . . . screams still
tear apart our conscience.
The graves
lie open, with many questions on their tongues.
The entrance to Kufr Qasim is still
terrified at the horror of that hellish night.
Oh, my bereft people,
all your children, all of them,
are in the core of my being . . .
I hate crying,
I hate kneeling at graves, while the butcher
pulls the fields out from under me
and offers my house to the wind.
Oh, the people who I love, beware!
The spotted serpent thirsts
ever for blood.

1964

1   Kufr Qasim [aka, Kafr Qasim]: A Palestinian village where Israeli
    border guards massacred 49 farm workers on their return from their
    fields unaware of a curfew imposed on the Arab population in Israel
    on October 29, 1956, the Eve of the Suez War, the invasion of Egypt
    by Israel, Britain and France.

Salem Jubran

ON NATIVE AMERICANS[1]

Flowers on your graves, America,
dancing and songs on corpses;
nothing is left of you except movies
evoking laughter . . . and tears.
Yes, my dead brothers, evoking laughter . . . and tears.
The farms of the settlers extend in all directions
large, fertile, green.
The factories of the settlers, they destroy the world
with their noise,
pollute the skies.
What can I say, brothers?
Nothing is left of you except movies
evoking laughter . . . and tears.

May God have mercy upon you,
death to the civilization that
survives on destruction . . . and blood . . .

1964

1 The text of this poem is as it appeared in Yusuf al-Khatib's *Diwan al-Watan al-Muhtall* (Anthology of the Occupied Homeland), pages 541–542, 1968. It differs from the version in S. Jubran's *Complete Works*.

SAFAD[1]

I am a stranger, ah, Safad,
and you are a stranger too.
The houses say, "Welcome,"
but its inhabitants order me, "Go away."

Why are you roaming the streets,
oh, Arab? Why?
When you cast your greetings,
no one returns the *salaams*.[2]
Your people were once here,
but they departed . . . no one remained.

Upon my lips – a funeral of dawn –
in my eyes
the bitterness of the lion's humiliation.
Farewell,
Farewell, Safad!

1965

1 Safad: a historical town in in Northern Palestine, north of Lake
  Tiberias (Sea of Galilee), with a mixed population of Arabs and Jews
  before 1948.
2 *salaam*: Arabic for greetings.

SONGS FROM THE PRISON[1]

-1-

The Opening of an Account

This is the first night.
Outside, the sound of rain.
From an opening in my window, I catch in the dark
the phantom of a palm tree.

The cold shoots needles,
the blankets, spittle and putrescene.
Silence: I curse its hollow sound.
I am alone in the prison, a captive.
Alone, alone,
how deep the waves of loneliness.
Alone at night I think,
whisper, sing, remember:
My path?
How silly of you, the enemies of pathways!
……………………………………………………
……………………………………………………
This is my first night,
not my last.

-2-

Shame

To the policeman who told me while I was handcuffed,
'now you can write poetry.'

The iron shackles bind my hands,
the sun rests on my forehead
before it sets . . .

The face is the same, his eyes grow into snakes:
"Greetings, Salim!
Are you back at the station again?
Do you still hate the Jews?
How long have you been here?
The court? The case of Deir Hanna?[2]
Nothing arouses poetry as much as adversity.
Recite some poems to them, your fellow inmates."

You who hate with malicious eyes and conscience;
I will tolerate all the chains,
I will recite my poems to the whole prison,
to all people, in all quarters and lanes.
The chains that bind my hands: a shame surely burning my
    conscience,
but the shame does not belong to me.
It is yours, despicable authority.
It is yours, you criminal police!

-3-

To Yafa of Nazareth[3]

You distributed to the prisoners, when you won your case,
two packs of cigarettes,
sang songs of struggle,
poked fun at the jailer and the chains.
My people outside the prison,
a tumultuous sea, roaring waves.
Oh, you red Yaffa! I kiss your winsome face
What good tidings follow good news!

This is the yield of the first harvest.
May you have strong forearms, my people,
for the fields promise good returns.

1964

1 This poem was taken from *Diwan al-Watan al-Muhtal* by Yusuf al-Khatib.
2 Deir Hanna, a Palestinian village in Lower Galilee. The reference is to a demonstration by Arab citizens that broke out without the Israeli authorities' approval, resulting in the arrest of its organizers. (Personal communication, 5 October 2014 with Sleman Jubran, the poet's brother.)
3 Yafa of Nazareth, an Arab village in Lower Galilee near the city of Nazareth, home to Palestinians from nearby villages displaced by Israel in the 1948 War. For decades, it was the bastion of the Arab Communist Party members including those in its elected city council.

THE HERALD OF WIND AND RAIN

You can uproot the trees
from the mountain in my village
in the moon's embrace.
You can bulldoze the houses in my village,
leaving no trace of them.
You can seize my *rababa*[1]
burn it, cutting its string.

You can . . . you can,
but you will never stifle my tunes,
for I am the lover of the land,
the minstrel of wind and rain.

1970

1 *rabab* or *rababa*: A stringed musical instrument, usually with one or
   two strings, resembling the fiddle.

THE REFUGEES' WINTER

Beyond the menacing borders, my homeland
is still awake, waiting for me.
In my thoughts are the land,
and its returning summer,
and my house.

Tomorrow winter will come,
wind will blow,
rain will fall,
and it will get cold; even the trees will get cold.
Everyone in the universe knows
that somewhere on earth they have a home.
Even dogs, everyone knows
they have a place of refuge in life,
even if only in a wooden crate near a house.
I continue, my friends and family continue
to live in hope,
beyond the degrading night of exile,
giving hope to the stars when we return
for the perfumes of Jaffa,[1]
the Carmel of Haifa,[2]
the luscious grapes of Galilee,
and the dry summer breeze that blows
gently on evening gatherings on rooftops.

Tomorrow winter will arrive,
Oh, the tomorrow of chill and storms
and the ice of lifeless conscience!
Tomorrow winter will come,
and my people of the diaspora
intone chants in the wasteland.

1964

1 Jaffa (Yafa, in Arabic) was a major orange-exporting city, thus the
  reference to orange blossoms.
2 Carmel is a coastal range of mountains in Palestine/Israel, on which
  the city of Haifa is located.

THE SLAUGHTERED VILLAGE

Blood, blood, blood:
as if the soil cannot grow vegetation
without blood.
Flesh piled upon flesh . . . and carnage
sharpen the beast's hunger for destruction.
The young
walk terrified between fire and dust,
as if black daggers had mutilated
their mothers' breasts in front of them,
yes, their mothers' breasts.
Their hearts!
They murmur "water".
But from whom?
From the skies, oh, little ones!
Even the doves flew away from hell,
even the doves flew away!

1975

THE TENT GENERATION

No matter how much I smile, lodged in my eyes
is the sadness of flowers on graves,
and the loss of cedar trees still standing
among the ruins in the villages of my blighted homeland
engulfed in bitter silence.

Has history torn apart a people like mine
and seized
a homeland, casting her people to the winds?
My homeland has gone to sleep beyond the sighs of the
   horizon,
my eyes are black, not by birth,
but in them the shadows of tents.
My lips are not those of a young man
yearning for women,
but for a dry loaf of bread.
Begging has dried them up . . . begging has dried them up.

My beloved homeland,
you are the only parent left to me.
Do you know who I am?
Yesterday, my father died,
and we buried him in exile.
He left behind only a photograph,

and a story of a glorious youth.
He lived his life in you, but died an exile,
bequeathing me banishment and love for you.

You talk of peace,
while here I am a branch without a root,
a mere covering raised up in the vast open air.
I am of a generation, growing, multiplying in tents;
hear it well:
yes, growing, multiplying in tents!
You leave behind crumbs on your dining table,
but let me go to sleep hungry, thirsty.
Woe to history!
We are the generation of tents.

1965

TO A VISITOR

Before you came the dome of the sky was yellow
the day was dark,
my night, all of it,
yearned after a world enveloped in secrets.
I was singing, tired, and alone,
singing poetry to the wastelands until you came,
and suddenly my window
smiled for the sun and welcomed it,
and my wall bloomed with flowers.

c. 1964

TO EVE

My Lady Eve:
without you I was but a prisoner
yawning in Paradise,
good for nothing but digestion,
sleep,
and repeating prayers,
short of breath, day and night.
Thank you, my Lady Eve.
I am happy to be called an outcast of Paradise
since for me Paradise is where you are!
Without you, all lands are uninhabitable.
Without you, all earthly gardens, a desert.

c. 1975

TO JEAN-PAUL SARTRE[1]

If a child were murdered, and his murderers tossed
his body in the mud,
would you be angry? What would you say?
I am a son of Palestine,
I die every year,
get killed every day,
every hour.
Come, behold the shades of ugliness,
all kinds of sights,
least horrible of which is my blood flowing.
Speak up:
What has caused your sudden indifference?
What, nothing to say?

1970

1 Sartre was vehemently opposed to France's colonization of Algeria,
  yet he was silent on Israel's harsh colonial policies toward Palestine.

Salem Jubran

WHATEVER IT WISHES

Galilee¹ was composed of people,
soil, vegetation and water.
And when I was denied visitation
Galilee became paradise,
and its population gods.
Even its night turned into dawn.
I say to those little Caesars:
How feeble you are!
You may restrict my movements,
but my heart is so deeply in love with my homeland
that it can visit any place it wishes,
can do whatever it will.

1970

1 Galilee: The northern part of Palestine, called al-Jalil in Arabic.

WITHOUT MEDALS

The oppressed learn how to steal
even drowsiness
from the eyes of their tormentors,
how to storm fortresses
to tell those who are imprisoned a thousand times
that redemption will come tomorrow.
If interrogated, keep silent.
If tortured,
spit in the eyes of those crucifying you.

The oppressed learn how to pay
for heroism
a daughter who has never dreamt of anything but her
    wedding,
who never mastered anything but braiding her hair
and a rose-age boy learning how to read,
who memorizes poems and beautiful stories.
The oppressed learn
how to master heroism.

The oppressed learn how
to make food from the soil, from the stones
of the homeland,
just like Christ's fish,

glorious, proud palaces from caves in the mountains.
Each rebellious place becomes in their eyes
a shrine of victory, or a monument.
They continue their march.
Their spilt blood hallows more sacrifices
for the birth of a new dawn.

The oppressed learn how to steal
even drowsiness
from the eyes of their tormentors,
how to offer the impossible
to be free in their homeland,
where there is neither dark night nor shackles.

1964

Zeinab Habash
(1943–)

EVA STAHL

"Eva was not an Arab.
She only was a human being with her eyes open,
who knew the meaning of our cause.
Suddenly Eva was wounded;
the honor of the revolution, oh, Eva
is a gift to your eyes."

Eva Stahl[1]
a song embracing a song!
I see in your kind hands
flocks of wild birds,
I see in your feet
haystacks of wheat to be reaped;
I see in your green eyes
bouquets of red roses,
I see in your green eyes
lush forests of tall palms
and hills of rosy-pink rocks;
in your eyes I see my homeland,
in your eyes I see a million skies;
in your eyes I see my flag,
in your eyes volcanoes
erupting fire
and blood.

Oh, Eva Stahl,
Isis of Palestine,
from your arms they took Osiris,
from your guts they took Horus,
from your limbs they took an arm and a foot,
from the light of the smile in your dreamy eyes
they spun a sail for death.
Please tell us Eva:
How, by God, did they drive
the nails of hatred into your palms?
How did they snatch the bandage
from your hands
while the body, wounded, was burdened with grief?

Oh, Eva,
sorrow it is to bear the sorrow of children,
the orphans!
Sorrow to bear all sins of the world!
Sorrow the tumult of time!
Sorrow to hold in our hands
the blood of martyrs!
Sorrow to be buried, oh, Eva,
without a shroud!
Sorrow to live in a land
without a homeland.
But the revolution predicts
a Christ who will gather the kidnapped and the dispersed.
The revolution foretells
a Christ who will heal souls
and restore light to blind eyes.

The revolution, oh Eva,
has become Mary,
and the revolutionaries, all revolutionaries
are now sons of the Virgin.

1976

1 Eva Stahl, a volunteer Swedish nurse who married a Palestinian refugee in Lebanon. Her husband was martyred during the 1976 siege of Tel al-Za'atar Camp by the Kata'ib (the Lebanese Maronite Christians Phalangist forces), the rightist militia organization Guards of Cedars, and other rightist Lebanese militias with the support of the Syrian Army. More than three thousand Palestinians, children, women and men, were killed. Stahl lost her unborn child, a foot and an arm while performing her job as a nurse with the Palestinians.

KUFR QASIM

*"Kufr Qasim, no longer that sleepy, sedate village
in the bosom of Palestine, has grown large and
become a homeland, a symbol."*

They decimated
Kufr Qasim,
slaughtered her sons in her lap
stole her bracelets
and rings.
They hanged her,
Kufr Qasim,
from an old sycamore tree
they hanged her,
and from the tears in her eyes
nurtured crimes.
She was like a kiss on the lips,
Kufr Qasim;
a rose in the leaves of a palm tree,
a smile on the face of a little girl
her bosom was a dovecote!
You did not die, Kufr Qasim,
you became wounded truth

the wound grew, slaking the thirst;
of the entire garden,
its buds nursed on this wound
until satiety.

1976

Muhammad al-Qaisi
(c. 1945–2003)

Muhammad al-Qaisi

EMMAUS, THE BRIDE

From ashes men are born, oh, Emmaus,[1]
from destroyed huts.
Your soil is mixed with blood blooms,
yet bears fragrance still.
Their scent remains in the air lingering
on the remnants of walls, oh, my beloved,
and the terrace.
Oh, Emmaus, you tortured one,
do you know, oh, Bride,
do you know about our exiled birds,
coming like wind, thunder, and rain
carrying the cure for your wound in their beaks?
Watch during dark nights:
their flocks come toward you.
Oh, Emmaus, the slain,
oh, Emmaus, the slain,
the spear has not broken yet,
the spear has not broken yet.

1999

1 Emmaus, a Palestinian village of about two thousand people in the
   Latrun Valley, near the city of Ramla (now Israeli) and Jerusalem, was
   depopulated of its Arab inhabitants by the Israeli forces in the 1967
   Arab-Israeli June War.

REEM AND THE WOUND

The little girl asks me,
her little fingers of innocence wounding me –
she says:
"Uncle . . .
where is your house?"
Oh, God, you little bird,
who changed children's games into torture
so that they ask questions in perplexity?
If I were to utter an answer,
how would you understand it, my little one?
My house is over there, on the horizon, bleeding
in our vanquished land,
a little thrush crying at its window,
crying for us,
crying for all our people to visit their homes.

1999

Mahmoud al-Najjar
(1958–)

HOMELAND

My lifelong dream has been
to live in a land
called homeland.
They said: God's world is spacious,
and has ample space for strangers,
and they may have a dwelling there.
My ribs replied, trembling
from humiliation and weakness:
"A delusion! Never have I experienced warmth
since leaving my homeland."

c. 2010

A WILL

My son,
when I die at last,
draped in sorrow
and many defeats;
when my back appears shattered
and my heart broken;
when my pitiful self vanishes from life,
when the earth consumes my corpse
and my features vanish
after a bitter end,
someday come and scatter
roses for my soul
and utter a brief phrase:
Jerusalem is captive no more.

c. 2014

Yousef al-Deek
(1959–)

ABBAS'S STATE

He who does not get a pain in the ass
or see how the monkey skulks around,
let him step inside the State of Abbas.

This State is tame –
no authority in this "Authority".
If a thief does not attend his court case,
they replace him with his neighbor and wife
for the bird's twittering on the telephone wires
may sound like "Hamas"!
Our brand of justice extends to all creatures
making the monkey like its owner,
the crook . . . like the policeman,
our extinct mammoth of a Council
like a declaration of bankruptcy.
Thanks be to God.
After our humiliation . . . labor pain . . . slumber,
we sneezed out . . . a Head of a State!
Oh, people: let us have the State!

2008

OSLO

All I need . . .
is half a tongue
to tell the whole truth
But . . .
I need six cluster bombs
to blow up the signatures and the hands writing them
and the Accords . . . !

1994

Rita Odeh
(1960–)

CHRISTMAS MISGIVINGS

I walk full of your delicious revelations,
among hundreds of exhausted faces
burdened with anxiety,
rushing at dusk
to the Christmas tree and the whining of a stove,
but then I realize that your heart alone
 is my homeland!

The chants of Fayrouz are booming[1]
from a loudspeaker:
"Glory to God in the Highest."
My heart throbs, repeating:
"And on Earth, occupation
and hearts thirsting for joy."

Bells peal
penetrating the Jerusalem mist
like drums of war,
and I see specters of planes,
spewing hatred from the sky.
And Fayrouz chants:
"Snow, snow,

rain down blessings, love and snow."
Anxiety piles up
in the manger of my heart.

The rain is light, light.
And on the Via Dolorosa hunger and thirst
continue to lay their siege
and dream about the prophecy of peace.

Fayrouz's voice continues to pierce the bones:
"Snow! Snow!"
I wrap myself with determination,
promising
to remain faithful to our love,
eternally,
after the billows of love raged
on the rocks of my heart
and it was splintered,
bent.
It then recited the Sura of Light[2]
and fell like a fish into your sea,
content, satisfied.

You, my stranger,
hunkering in the snow of dispersal
you are my Shahrayar every night[3]
listening to my tales,

bitter and pure,
the aridness of exile and the ache of identity.
Until I occupy the throne
of your affections,
Christmas Eve is
 ever the same.

2003

1 Fayrouz: Lebanese singer considered the Edith Piaf of the Arab world.
   She sings secular and religious songs.
2 Chapter 24 in the Qur'an.
3 Shahrayar: the fictional misogynist king in *One Thousand and One Nights.*

Marwan Makhoul
(1979-)

DAILY POEMS

After the country had fallen into a well,
it fell upon us after sixty years
to hoist the rope slightly, then let it drop again.
Only thus does hope build on patience.

There are matters I don't comprehend.
I am not Israeli,
nor am I a full Palestinian.

My homeland is a ravished young woman
whom I shall wed.

My grandfather told me:
Palestine is a past tense defective verb.
My father said:
but it is a present tense verb.
I say, as a fighter jet shrieks close to me:
my grandfather is right,
and so is my father.

2011

Marwan Makhoul

ON THE TEL AVIV TRAIN

On the train to Tel Aviv
I saw her,
a Russian, tender, fragrant, like a mint patch!
All of Moscow was hers
as well, as a child looking
Levantine.

An Ethiopian went in the same car
staring at the faces of passengers.
He stared until he became bored,
then he began to look out the window
at the ruins of an Arab village, unconcerned.

A worker from the so-called "newcomers".
Full of energy . . . in a short while he'll disembark
from the train for his job in a company
that just announced his dismissal.

To my right sat a Jew,
a Moroccan, he told me about himself

131

until he puzzled out my accent.
He kept on talking
but with the person . . . to his right.

Then . . . I got off at the nearest station
for my poem had come to an end.

2008

BIOGRAPHIES

MU'IN BSEISO (1926-1984)

Born and raised in Gaza, Bseiso completed his secondary education in 1948 and pursued his education at the American University in Cairo. During his stay in Egypt, he was jailed twice due to his affiliation with the Communist Party. Upon graduation, he worked as a teacher in Iraq and Gaza, as well as a journalist in Damascus and Beirut. He was involved in international organizations, working, for example, as Deputy Editor-in-Chief of the publication of the Afro-Asian Writers Association, *The Lotus*.

His first poem was published in 1946 in *al-Hurriyya* [Liberty], a magazine that appeared in Jaffa, Palestine. Bseiso authored several poetry collections, plays, and prose works. His poetry has been translated into many foreign languages.

YOUSEF AL-DEEK (1959-)

Born in Baqa al-Gharbiyya, Palestine, al-Deek studied law and worked in the banking sector from 1982 until 2002. He is a member of several writers' associations including The Jordan Writers' Association, The General Association of Arab Literati and Writers, and The Palestinian Association of Literati and Writers. al-Deek has published three collections of poetry, including *Tuqus al-Nar* [Rituals of Fire] (1986), *Tafasil Saghira* 'ala Nuhas al-Qalb [Little Details about the Heart's Copper] (2005), and a joint volume in Arabic and French, entitled *Shu'ara' min Bilad al-Sham* [Poets from the Levant]. He also published a novel, *Tanhidat al-'Asa, Talwihat al-Junun* [The Sigh of Grief and A Hint of Madness] (2011).

ZEINAB HABASH (1943–)

Born in Beit Dajan, near Jaffa, Habash's family was the last family expelled from Jaffa by the Israeli army; subsequently, the family moved to Nablus, where Habash studied at an UNRWA school. She and her family, active in Palestinian revolutionary activities, suffered many blows at the hands of the Israeli army, including the death of two brothers and a nephew, as well as her own arrest in 1967–68 by the Israeli occupation forces. These experiences affected the content of her poetry.

Habash pursued her university education in Damascus (1961–65) and went on to teach English in schools in Palestine. In 1982 she obtained an MA in education administration and supervision from Bir Zeit University, Ramallah. Habash has been influenced by such Arab poets as Fadwa Tuqan and Badr Shakir al-Sayyab, as well as the English Romantic poets Shelley, Keats and Coleridge, to whom she was exposed through the course of her studies in English literature. She has published poems in Jerusalem's literary journal *al-'Ufuq al-Jadid*, and Haifa's newspaper *al-Ittihad*. She has published several poetry collections including *al-Jurh al-Filastini wa Bara'im al-Dam* [The Palestinian Wound and the Blossoms of Blood] and *La Taquli Mata 'akhi*, [Do not Say My Brother Died]. She has also published one novel, *al-Farasha wa al-'Ukhtubut*, [The Butterfly and the Octopus]; and several short story collections.

RASHID HUSSEIN (1936–1977)

Born in Masmas, a village in central Palestine, Hussein completed his secondary education in Nazareth in 1954. He then taught for three years in a village school but was expelled in 1958 by the Israeli authorities due to his political activism.

He worked as editor of several Israeli-sponsored journals and magazines, including *al-Fajr* (until 1961), *al-Mirsad*, and *al-Musawwar*. In 1965 he left Israel for the USA where he worked odd jobs for a brief time. In 1971 he moved to Beirut, making brief visits to Damascus, and Cairo. In 1972 he worked in Damascus as a translator from Hebrew into Arabic at the Palestine Studies Center, established by Habib Qahwaji, who was expelled from Israel in 1968 for his political activism. Eventually Hussein was himself expelled from Syria, returning to the USA, where he led a bohemian life. He died in an apartment fire in New York in February 1977.

He is credited with several poetry collections, including *Ma' al-Fajr* [At Dawn], published in Nazareth in 1957 and also in Cairo in the same year, and *Sawarikh* [Rockets] (1958). In addition, he translated into Arabic selections from the Jewish poet Chaim Bialik.

SALEM JUBRAN (1941–2011)

Born in Northern Galilee, Jubran completed his secondary education in 1962 in Kufr Yasif, and graduated from Haifa University in 1972. During his university years, he worked in journalism, eventually becoming editor of *al-Jadid* magazine, and Editor-in-Chief of *al-Ghad*, the Communist Youth organ. Jubran also held the post of editor-in-chief of *al-Ittihad* daily that was published in Haifa. He founded *al-Thaqafa* magazine and edited it until his death in 2011.

Jubran wrote many articles for Arabic newspapers and journals outside Israel, including *al-Tariq*, *al-'Adab*, and *Sawt Filastin*. He published three poetry collections: *Kalimat min al-Qalb* [Words from the Heart] (1971) in Akka (Acre), *Qasa'id Laysat Muhaddadat al-'Iqama* [Poems Not Restricted to a Place] (1970) in Beirut, and *Rifaq al-Shams* [Friends of the Sun] (1975) in Nazareth.

YOUSSEF AL-KHATIB (1931–2011)

Born in Doura, near Hebron, where he completed his secondary education in the town school, al-Khatib attended the University of Damascus, graduating in law in 1955. He worked in many radio stations in several Arab countries, and in the Arabic section of the Dutch Radio in The Netherlands. He published six poetry collections, including *al-'Uyun al-Dham'a' li- al-Nur* [Thirsty Eyes to Light] (1955), *'A'idun* [Returning] (1958), *Wahat al-Jahim* [Oasis of Hell] (1964).

MAHMOUD AL-NAJJAR (1958–)

Born in Gaza Strip, al-Najjar earned his BA in Arabic from the University of Jordan, Amman in 1983. At this writing, he heads the Organization of Poets Without Borders and is involved in several civic societies. He has worked as a teacher and journalist, and is the author of several poetry collections, including *Rasas min Huruf* [Bullets of letters], *Ishti'al li-Intifa al-'akhar* [Flames to Extinguish the Other], and *Maraya al-Ruh* [Mirrors of the Soul].

MARWAN MAKHOUL (1979–)

Born in Bqay'a in Upper Galilee, Makhoul practises literary writing and poetry in addition to his work as a civil engineer. He has participated in many festivals and poetry readings in many countries around the world. Several of his poems have been translated into English, Italian, Hebrew, Turkish, and Serbian. He earned the Mahmoud Darwish Award during the Jerusalem Capital for Arab Culture Festival in 2009. His first play, *Mish Safinat Nuh* [Not Noah's Ship], was awarded the best theatrical work in Akka (Acre) Festival for Theater in 2009. His poem 'Arus al-Jalil [The Bride of Galilee] (2005) was adapted into a documentary film that earned him the second prize in the World Documentary Film Festival in Haifa in 2006.

RITA ODEH (1960-)

Born in Nazareth, Palestine, where she currently lives and teaches, Odeh earned Bachelor of Arts degree in English and Comparative Literature from Haifa University. She has authored several poetry collections, including *Thawra 'ala al-Samt* [Revolt against Silence] (1994), *Yawmiyyat Ghajariyya 'Ashiqa* [Diary of a Gypsy Woman Lover] (2001), *Man la Ya'rifu Rita* [Who does not Know Rita] (2003), as well as a collection of short stories *'Ana Jununuka* [I am your Madness] (2009), three electronic novels, and one e-book of Haiku, which reflects her active blogging. Her poetry has been published in several international publications.

MUHAMMAD AL-QAISI (c. 1945–2003)

Born in Kufr 'Ana, a village located between Lod [aka Lidd] and Jaffa, al-Qaisi moved with his family when they were expelled from their homes during the 1948 Arab-Israeli War. The family settled in al-Jalazon Refugee Camp, near Ramallah. He obtained a Bachelor of Arts degree in Arabic in 1971 from Beirut Arab University. Living in several countries thereafter, he worked in teaching, journalism, and radio and television.

His poetry has earned him many awards. al-Qaisi has published thirteen poetry collections, including *Raya fi al-Rih* [A Banner in the Wind], and *al-Hidad Yaliq bi-Haifa* [Mourning Becomes Haifa], in addition to poetry collections for children, and several prose works. He has also published an autobiography titled *'Abariq al-Ballour:Yawmiyyat Sahrawiyya* [Glass Jugs: Desert Diaries].

SAMIH AL-QASIM (1939-2014)

Born in Zarqa, Jordan where his father was an officer in the Jordanian Army at the time, al-Qasim moved with his family when they returned to their native village Ramah, near Akka (Acre). Upon completing his studies, he became a teacher. Due to his political activism against the Israeli Military Rule over the Palestinian Arab citizens of Israel (1984-1966), al-Qasim was expelled from his job, jailed several times, and put under house arrest for long stretches.

al-Qasim is considered one of the leading contemporary Palestinian poets and is credited with several poetry collections, including *Mawakib al-Shams* [Parades of the Sun] (1958), *'Aghani al-Durub* [Songs on the Road] (1964), and *Dukhkhan al-Barakin* [Smoke of the Volcanos]. He has also authored many books in prose as well as plays. His autobiography, titled *'Innaha Mujarrad Minfadaha* [Life is Only an Ashtray] appeared in 2011.

HARUN HASHIM RASHEED (1927-2020)

Rasheed was born in Gaza and is known as the Resistance Poet, due to the theme of resistance in his poetry. He worked in teaching and also in media and represented Palestine at the Arab League for several years. Among Palestinian poets, he is noted for using the vocabulary of "return" in his poems. His first collection, titled *Ma* al-Ghuraba' [Among Strangers] records the loss of his homeland and the impact of the 1948 *Nakba* catastrophe on Palestinians.

Rasheed is the author of more than twenty collections of poetry, including plays in verse that have been performed in several Arab countries. He authored one novel. All his writings focus on the Palestinian *Nakba*. Some of his poems have been put to music and sung by the celebrated Lebanese singer Fayrouz, including the poem in this collection. Rasheed has won many literary awards from several Arab countries.

FADWA TUQAN (1917-2003)
Tuqan was born in Nablus, Palestine, into a notable, yet conservative family that did not provide her with formal education. Her brother, the renowned Palestinian poet Ibrahim Tuqan, was instrumental in exposing her to poetry, classical Arab culture and the English language. In her earlier years, she produced sentimental, lyric poetry.

As a result of the 1967 Arab-Israeli War which resulted in the occupation of the whole of Palestine in addition to Arab lands belonging to Syria, Lebanon, and Egypt by Israel, Tuqan turned her poetry to issues relating to the Palestinian cause and its acts of resistance against the Israeli occupation.

Tuqan has published several collections of poetry, in addition to her two-volume autobiography, *Rihla Jabaliyya S'aba* [A Difficult Trip into the Mountains] and *al-Rihla al-'As'ab* [The More Difficult Trip].

ASMA RIZQ TUBI (1905-1983)
Born in Nazareth, Tubi edited the women's page in *Palestine*, the newspaper issued in Jaffa, Palestine before the 1948 *Nakba*.

She was interested in women's issues and active in the Women's Union in Akka (Acre) (1929-48), especially Christian Orthodox Young Women Union and YWCA. She was forced to emigrate to Beirut, where she continued her work in journalism and broadcasting. In Beirut, Tubi edited the women's page in *Kul Shay'* newspaper and *al-Ahad* magazine. She has a poetry collection titled *Hubbi al-Kabir* [My Great Love] printed in Beirut (1972), and several other books dealing with women's issues.

ABDEL WAHAB ZAHIDA (1939-2010)
Little is known about this poet, who originated in Hebron, Palestine. Zahida worked as a reporter for the Israeli Television on the West Bank in the 1970s and 1980s while remaining committed to the Palestinian cause. Most of his poetry concerns Palestine and the *Nakba* but it also takes on corrupt Arab rulers, of whom he is a severe critic. He vehemently opposed the 1978 Israeli-supported plan, "The Association of Hebron District Villages", of Rabitat Qura Muhafazat al-Khalil, whose goal was to undermine the PLO as the representative of the Palestinian people.

TAWFIQ ZAYYAD (1929-1994)
Born in Nazareth, Palestine, Zayyad completed his secondary school in that city. He studied Russian Literature in Moscow, involved himself in the Palestinian national movement, and joined the Communist Party in which he was an active member. He was also elected to the Israeli Knesset, representing the Israeli Communist Party, Rakah. Zayyad worked in journalism and was elected mayor of Nazareth in 1978 until his death in a car accident in 1994.

Zayyad is considered one of the pioneering resistance poets, along with of Hanna Abu Hanna and Salem Jubran. His poetry portrays the suffering and resistance of Palestinians against the Israeli occupation. Besides several poetry collections that include *'Ashuddu 'ala 'Ayadikum* [I Clasp your Hands] (1966), *'Ughniyat al-Thawra wa al-Ghadab* [Songs of the Revolution and Anger] (1969), and *Kalimat Muqatila* [Fighting Words] (1970), he wrote essays and short stories. His deep interest in Palestinian folklore led to his publication *'An al-'Adab al-Sha'bi al-Filastini* [Palestinian Folklore Literature] (1970). He also translated Russian literature and the poetry of the Turkish poet Nazim Hikmat into Arabic. His own poetry has been translated into many foreign languages.

MOHAMMED SAWAIE

Mohammed Sawaie, Professor of Arabic at the University of Virginia, USA, is the author and editor of internationally renowned studies in English and Arabic. A lifelong love for the Arabic language has made him a global authority on the sociolinguistic, historical, and grammatical aspects of Arabic. His *Fundamentals of Arabic Grammar* (London and New York, 2014, Routledge) has majorly contributed to the teaching of Arabic in North America. *The Tent Generations, Palestinian Poems* is the latest title in a bibliography of over ten books in English and Arabic, which can be found in libraries worldwide, including *Linguistic Variation and Speaker's Attitudes: A Sociolinguistic Study of Some Arabic Dialects* (1994), and *Arabic-Speaking Migrants in the United States and Canada: a Bibliographical Guide with Annotation* (1985). His works also include *Min Fursan al-'Arabiyya fi al-Qarn al-Tasi' 'Ashar* [Studies in 19th Century Arabic] (Beirut, 2017) al-Mu'assassa al-'Arabiyya li al-Dirasat wa al-Nashr; *al-Hadatha wa Mustalahat al-Nahda al-*Arabiyya [Modernity and Nineteenth Century Arabic Lexicography: A Case Study of Ahmad Faris al-Shidyaq] (Beirut, 2013) al-Mu'assassa al-'Arabiyya li al-Dirasat wa al-Nashr; *'Azmat al-Mustalah al-Lughawi fi al-Qarn al-Tasi' 'Ashar* [Crisis of Terminology in Arabic in the 19th Century] (Damascus, 1999) Institut français d'Études arabes de Damas; in addition to dozens of articles and other works in Arabic and English.

Artist of the front cover painting
"Melancholic Homeland"

TOUFIC ABDUL-AL

Palestinian artist, sculptor, and poet Toufic Abdul-Al (1938–2002) was born in Acre, and was forced to leave Palestine in 1948, and live the rest of his life in Lebanon. His distinctive style enriched Palestinian cultural heritage with a varied spectrum of exceptional works as he joined the top ranks of artists in the post-*Nakba* Palestinian art scene. He participated in numerous exhibitions in the Arab world, with his work recognized through many awards.

Banipal thanks the Abdul-Al family for their kind permission to reproduce a section of Toufic Abdul-Al's painting of 1985 entitled "Melancholic Homeland" (oil on canvas, 50x60cm) for the front cover of *The Tent Generations, Palestinian Poems*.

GLOSSARY

Abbas, Mahmoud The President of the Palestinian National
Authority since 2005.

Allahu Akbar   A phrase literally meaning 'God is greater than
all' used in various contexts as in call to prayer,
as an expression of wonderment or sarcastically
as a sign of disapproval.

Allenby Bridge   Built over the River Jordan, this bridge links
Palestine and Jordan. Named after General
Edmund Henry Allenby, who defeated the
Ottoman forces in Jerusalem in 1917. It is also
known as King Hussein Bridge by the
Jordanian authorities, and al-Karama Bridge by
the Palestinian National Authority.

Church of the Nativity Church in the Palestinian City of
Bethlehem, the location where Christians
believe Christ was born.

Coptic Monastery One of several monasteries of the Christian
Copts of Egypt in Jerusalem.

Dome of the Rock An Islamic edifice in the Old City of
Jerusalem built in 691 CE.

Galilee   The northern regions of Palestine / Israel; called
al-Jalil in Arabic.

Golden Gate   Since medieval times, a sealed gate in the
eastern part of the Ottoman wall surrounding
the City of Old Jerusalem.

Hamas   One of the Palestinian organizations resisting
the Israeli occupation.

Hamza   A man's name, signifying bravery.

Horus   Ancient Egyptian deity in the form of a falcon.
Each eye of Horus has various meanings,
including power, quintessence, and healing.

Jaffa	Ancient port Palestinian city on the Mediterranean, now in Israel. It was an important commercial and cultural center in Palestine until 1948, especially famous for exporting its eponymous oranges.
Khan al-Zayt	A well-known commercial street in Old Jerusalem, presumably where olive oil was traded historically.
Levant	Geographical regions east of the Mediterranean Sea, including, Greece, Lebanon, Palestine, and parts of Syria and Egypt.
Levantine	A native of the Levant regions.
The Lion's Gate	One of the gates of the old City of Jerusalem, located in the eastern Ottoman wall of the City
Lod [aka Lidd]	An old city in central Palestine / Israel
Najma Suq/ Souk	A market in Old Jerusalem.
Nakba	The Arabic term for the catastrophe that befell the Palestinians in 1948 resulting in the loss of their country to Israel.
Osiris	Ancient Egyptian god of the afterlife, the underworld; also the god of resurrection.
Oslo Accords	The 1993 agreement between Israel and the Palestine Liberation Organization (PLO) that established the Palestinian Authority.
Ramla	A city in central Palestine / Israel established in 716 CE by the Umayyad Caliph Sulaiman bin Abd-al-Malik for the Arab Army that conquered Greater Syria in 637 CE and eventually Egypt in 640 CE.
Reem	A woman's name.
Salwa	A woman's name.
State	The Palestinian National Authority.
Sura	A chapter of the Qur'an.
Temple	A Jewish place of worship in the Old City of Jerusalem.

ACKNOWLEDGMENTS

This work could not have been accomplished without support and help from many friends and colleagues. Cecilia F. Blewer witnessed this translation from its inception to its final stages. She often and considerably pointed out nuances of expressions that more aptly convey the intended meaning. Naomi Shihab Nye kindly read all poems, made valuable suggestions, and showed strong support for the project. William McDonald recited the poems out loud to hear the rhythm and test the proper fit of words and expressions. Fadia Suyoufi has read the translations and made several useful comment. Jessica Allison, and Lucine Taminian contributed towards making the translation more readable. Sherif Abdelkarim and Eric Stickley Calderwood read the introduction and made valuable suggestions. Barbara A. Brothers and Vivian Bishara McCormack were all along very supportive throughout the process.

I will be remiss if I do not offer sincere thanks to Samir Hajj who encouraged the project of translating Palestinian poetry into English from the inception of the idea. He was desirous of having the work of the poet from his Galilean Abilin village, the Israeli Palestinian George Najib Khalil, included in this collection. I beg him for forgiveness for not fulfilling his wish. Most importantly, Samir was helpful in putting me in contact with Professor Sleman Jubran, brother of poet Salem Jubran, whose splendid poems are now in the reader's hands. Sleman Jubran deserves gratitude and sincere thanks, not only for giving the family's permission to translate some of Salem's poetry, but also for his writings in general, especially on the literary scene among Palestinians under Israel and the latter's harsh treatment of Palestinian writers all along.

Khaled al-Masri deserves my sincere thanks for introducing my work to publisher Margaret Obank and Samuel Shimon, editor-in-chief of *Banipal*, and for his limitless endeavor to make sure this work sees the light. Joselyn Michelle Almeida copyedited the manuscript in most professional and supportive terms. She was exemplary in her support of this project, contributing to improvements at many levels across the Atlantic Ocean.

Many individuals at several institutions extended support to this project in their different ways and remain nameless. Chief among them are the employees of the Interlibrary Loan Department at University of Virginia's Alderman Library who were extremely helpful in obtaining material, particularly Palestinian poetry items that were not available in the library collection. The office of the Dean of Arts and Sciences granted me funds to travel to Beirut in Spring 2018 to search for material on Palestinian poetry. Employees of The German Institute for Oriental Research in Beirut (OIB) were most welcoming by facilitating access to materials in the Institute's library collection. I would like to single out Stefan Seeger for his warmth, friendship, and support for this project. Many others in different parts of the world contributed in their own ways, offering support, encouragement, and professional advice.

OTHER TITLES FROM BANIPAL BOOKS

The Stone Serpent, Barates of Palmyra's Elegy for Regina his Beloved by Nouri al-Jarrah. Translated from the Arabic by Catherine Cobham. ISBN: 978-1-913043-29-2 • 2022 • 160pp • Pbk & Ebook. Syrian poet al-Jarrah restores to life an ancient story of migrant Syrian life, love and freedom, discovered at Hadrian's Wall and Arabeia Roman Fort.

Things I Left Behind by Shada Mustafa. Translated from the Arabic by Nancy Roberts. ISBN: 978-1-913043-26-1 • 2022 • 144pp • Pbk & Ebook. This debut novel by a young Palestinian author is an innovative narrative of memory and pain, interrogating the "things" she left behind from her childhood in an occupied and divided land and family.

The Tent Generations, Palestinian Poems. Selected, introduced, and translated by Mohammed Sawaie. ISBN: 978-1-913043-18-6 • 2022 • 160pp • Pbk & Ebook. These Palestinian poets, most in English for the first time, bear witness, through their experiences of displacement, disapora and occupation, to the *Nakba* of 1948, 1967, 1973 and beyond.

Sarajevo Firewood by Saïd Khatibi. Translated from the Arabic by Paul Starkey. ISBN 978-1-913043-23-0 • 2021 • 320pp • Pbk & Ebook. A searing novel that explores the legacy of the recent histories, connections and civil wars of Algeria and Bosnia-Herzegovina and the traumatic experience of exile for so many.

Fadhil Al-Azzawi's Beautiful Creatures by Iraqi author Fadhil al-Azzawi. ISBN 978-1-913043-10-0 • 2021 • 152pp • Hbk, Pbk, Ebook. An open poetic work, written in defiance of the "sanctity of genre", translated from the Arabic by the author, and edited by Hannah Somerville.

The Madness of Despair by Ghalya F T Al Said. Translated from the Arabic by Raphael Cohen. ISBN: 978-1-913043-12-4 • 2021 • 256pp • Hbk, Pbk, Ebook. The first of the author's six novels to be published in English is a powerful saga of how psychological suffering and cultural displacement can upset the most ordinary of aspirations for life and love.

Poems of Alexandria and New York by Ahmed Morsi. Translated from the Arabic by Raphael Cohen. ISBN 978-1-913043-16-2 • 2021 • 126pp • Pbk & Ebook. First volume in English translation for renowned painter, art critic, and poet, comprising two of his many collections.

148

Mansi: A Rare Man in His Own Way by Tayeb Salih. Translated and introduced by Adil Babikir. ISBN 978-0-9956369-8-9 • Paperback & Ebook • 184pp • 2020. This affectionate memoir of Salih's irrepressible friend Mansi shows a new side to the author, known the world over for his classic novel *Season of Migration to the North*.

Goat Mountain by Habib Selmi.Translated from the Arabic by Charis Olszok. ISBN: 978-1-913043-04-9 • 2020 • Pbk & Ebook • 92pp. The well-known Tunisian author's debut novel, from 1988, now in English translation. "*I enjoyed this book. I liked its gloomy atmosphere, its strangeness . . . Eerie, funereal, and outstanding!*" – Jabra Ibrahim Jabra

The Mariner by Taleb Alrefai. Translated from the Arabic by Russell Harris. ISBN: 978-1-913043-08-7 • Pbk & Ebook • 160pp • 2020. A fictional re-telling of the final sea journey of famous Kuwaiti dhow shipmaster Captain Al-Najdi.

A Boat to Lesbos, and other poems by Nouri Al-Jarrah. Translated from the Arabic by Camilo Gómez-Rivas and Allison Blecker and illustrated with paintings by Reem Yassouf. ISBN: 978-0-9956369-4-1 • 2018 • Pbk • 120pp. The first book in English translation for this major Syrian poet, bearing passionate witness – through the eye of history, of Sappho and the travels of Odysseus – to Syrian families fleeing to Lesbos.

An Iraqi In Paris by Samuel Shimon. ISBN: 978-0-9574424-8-1 • Pbk • 282pp • 2016. Translated from the Arabic by Christina Philips and Piers Amodia with the author. Called by critics: "a gem of autobiographical writing", "a manifesto of tolerance", "a cinematographic odyssey".

Heavenly Life: Selected Poems by Ramsey Nasr. ISBN: 978-0-9549666-9-0 • 2010 • Pbk • 180pp. First English-language collection for Ramsey Nasr, Poet Laureate of the Netherlands 2009 & 2010. Translated from the Dutch by David Colmer. Introduced by Victor Schiferli with Foreword by Ruth Padel.

Knife Sharpener: Selected Poems by Sargon Boulus. The first English-language collection for the influential and innovative late Iraqi poet. ISBN: 978-0-9549666-7-6 • 2009 • Pbk • 154pp. Foreword by Adonis. Poems translated from the Arabic by the author. Plus tributes by fellow authors and Afterword by the publisher.

Shepherd of Solitude: Selected Poems by Amjad Nasser. Translated from the Arabic and introduced by Khaled Mattawa. ISBN: 978-0-9549666-8-3 • 2009 • Pbk • 186pp. First English-language collection for the late major Jordanian poet, poems selected from the years 1979 to 2004.

Mordechai's Moustache and his Wife's Cats, and other stories by short story maestro Mahmoud Shukair. ISBN: 978-0-9549666-3-8 • 2007 • Pbk • 124pp. Translated from the Arabic by Issa J Boullata, Elizabeth Whitehouse, Elizabeth Winslow and Christina Phillips. First major publication in English of Palestine's most original of storytellers.

A Retired Gentleman, & other stories by Issa J Boullata.
ISBN: 978-0-9549666-6-9 • 2007 • Pbk • 120pp. The Jerusalem-born author, scholar, and translator presents a rich medley of emigrant tales.

The Myrtle Tree by Lebanese Jad El Hage. ISBN: 978-0-9549666-4-5 • 2007 • Pbk • 288pp. "This remarkable novel, set in a Lebanese mountain village, conveys with razor-sharp accuracy the sights, sounds, tastes and tragic dilemmas of Lebanon's fratricidal civil war. A must read" – Patrick Seale.

Sardines and Oranges: Short Stories from North Africa. Introduced by Peter Clark. ISBN: 978-0-9549666-1-4 • 2005 • Pbk • 222pp. The 26 stories from Algeria, Egypt, Morocco, Sudan and Tunisia are by 21 authors, all translated from the Arabic, bar one, Mohammed Dib's from French.